Active Writing
Understand, practise, succeed

JULIA STRONG & KIM RICHARDSON

KEY STAGE 3 / YEAR **7**

Contents grid

Section 3 – Text structure/organisation	Section 4 – Sentence structure/organisation	Section 5 – Composing own text
R15, R4, R7 • Using timelines and time connectives	R12, R14, S1a, S3, R7 • Varying sentence structures • Using dialogue to tell stories	W6, S11, S15, W1, W2 W5, W7, W9, W6 • Writing a short story and portraying character
R13, R4, (Wr20), S8, S13b • Understanding and using paragraphs, linking text chronologically	S1b, S1c, S3 • Exploring subordinate clauses and punctuation	W1, W2, S8, S9, S12, S11 • Writing a recount text
R4, (Wr10) • Analysing and experimenting with how a text is organised and signposted	S6, S3 • Using pronouns and punctuation effectively	W1, W2, S8, S12, S11 • Writing an information text
S13c, W10, W12, S8, R4 • Organising and signposting a text logically • Understanding how to use paragraphs	S5, S13d, S1, S3, (W20) • Understanding the passive voice and complex sentences	W1, W2, W5, W12, S12, S13c, S5 • Writing an explanation using paragraphs and using the present tense and an informal 'voice'
S13d, W13 • Considering how to sequence and signpost instructions	R13, S4, S13d • Using appropriate terminology and tenses to write instructions	W10, W13, W1, (Wr8) • Writing directions clearly using visual and sound effects
R7, R13, S12, R15, S8, S9, S10, S11 • Using signposts to make writing cohesive	S3, S11, R12, R14, W15 • Using punctuation and varying sentence length and complexity for interest	W1, W3, W15, S8, S12, S11 • Writing a persuasive letter
S8, S9, S12, R15, R4, R7 • Identify opening and closing paragraphs • Structuring an argument text	S5, S11, R14 • Using the passive voice • Giving writing rhythm, impact and interest	W1, W3, W15, S12, S11, W16 • Writing an editorial, validating own argument
R4, R7, S12, S9, R7, R14, W17 • Structuring an advice text and using bullet points	S1, S3 • Exploring conditional sentences • Combining simple sentences to make complex ones	W1, W3, W17 • Writing a piece of informal advice
R7, R13, S12 • Identifying and understanding topic sentences	S9, S10, S4 • Using connectives	R4, W1, W2, S13f, S8, S9, S12 • Writing a discursive essay
R4, R7, S12 • Analysing the review structure	S2, (Wr6) • Using noun and noun phrases • Using the apostrophe	W1, W2, S8, S12, S11 • Writing an information text

Collins Active Writing 1 is a practical guide to all the different types of writing facing students in Year 7. It is structured to build up students' confidence as writers through learning from example. It helps students understand the varied features that make up effective writing, depending on its audience and purpose, and provides an interactive step-by-step approach to practising these features. Every unit builds towards an extended piece of writing in a different text type supported by peer evaluation and target setting.

How the book is organised

The units

The book has ten units focusing on the six non-fiction text types (recount, information, explanation, instruction, persuasion and discussion) and narrative that together cover the different purposes of writing. Argue, advise and review are also included as types of persuasive and discursive writing. The units are grouped under the triplet headings of the National Curriculum for English.

A unit has five sections reflecting the criteria used to assess writing.

Section 1 – How the text type works: This builds on students' prior knowledge and provides an overview of a particular type of text highlighting. Students analyse this text using annotation and a note-making tool called a **text skeleton**.

Section 2 – Composition and effect: This helps students learn from example by introducing a longer text that forms the basis of the work in Sections 2, 3 and 4. This time the focus is on audience and purpose, the way the writer has used different language features to create specific effects. Students will practise using these effects for themselves.

Section 3 – Text structure and organisation: This emphasises the structure of the main text and how the writer has linked sections and ideas within paragraphs. Using a text skeleton and sentence signposts, students will analyse the structure of the main text and plan a text of their own.

Section 4 – Sentence structure and punctuation: This focuses on the grammar and punctuation that is appropriate for the text type. Students will practise changing and developing sentences to add more variety to their writing.

Section 5 – Composing your own text: This delivers the main task of the unit and is the students' chance to write a longer piece in the text type. As they brainstorm ideas, and plan, draft and revise their own writing, students will draw on all the work they have done in Sections 1–4. To help students further, this section also provides plenty of reminders and support for the writing task.

The units are loosely linked by the theme of time (e.g. *How Long Will it Take?* in Unit A and *What is Time?* in Unit C) to show that it is not theme that generates a type of text, but audience and purpose.

The Exemplar section

At the back of the book are example responses for selected tasks in Sections 1 to 4. These are not intended as the 'only answer', but as a guide to show students how they might respond to the task. This icon **X** appears when there is an exemplar for a task.

When the **TR** icon appears next to a task, it indicates that in the Teacher's Book there is either a black-and-white version of the example text for annotation or a worksheet to support the task.

Tasks as building blocks

The tasks in each unit provide practice in the following vital skills for writing.

- **Learning from example** – identifying text features and their effects (see page 7)
- **Planning practice** – using text skeletons to help structure writing (see page 8) and using signposts to help guide the reader (see page 17)
- **Spinning sentences** – understanding how to structure sentences and punctuate them correctly (see page 18)
- **Targeted activities** – mini-writing tasks, supported by discussion, throughout allow practice in the language features explored (see page 20) building towards the main writing task at the end of each unit (see page 22).

Part of a model answer is often provided to help students tackle a task.

The class organisation for each task is shown by the following icons:

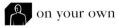 on your own   in pairs   in groups

The emphasis is on interactive tasks to maximise student understanding through focused paired and group work. This builds up to support independent writing. Only the teacher introductions and class feedback and presentations are whole-class activities.

Clear explanations

Explanations of vocabulary, grammar, structure and style features are outlined through the following.

- Typical features panel – listing the form and language features of each text type – see the first page of each unit.
- Grammar panel – explaining a grammar point clearly and providing examples.
- Glossary panel – defining tricky words in texts and explanations.
- Highlighted text – emphasising each language feature consistently for instant recognition. For example, students will always know that text highlighted in orange is a topic sentence while text highlighted in mauve is a time connective (see page 146).

How *Collins Active Writing* increases confidence for the test

Students' ability to write well for a wide range of audiences and purposes is all-important in gaining a high mark in the Year 7 optional tests and end of key stage test. *Collins Active Writing* helps students prepare in several ways.

- At the start of Sections 2 and 5, Test Watch panels **Test watch** list the skills students will need to develop for the test
- The main task in Section 5 acts as full-scale practice for the type of task students will meet in the test
- On-going formative assessment is provided by the pair evaluation task ▦ and the setting of own writing targets task ◎ at the end of Section 5. These are supported by copymasters in the Teacher's Resource
- A complete mock test with example answers related to the marking criteria is provided in the Teacher's Resource to refine students' test skills.

By using *Collins Active Writing 1* students will not only improve their writing skills and chances of success in the end of year tests, but will increase their confidence as writers.

A The Art of Narrative Writing

How narrative text works

AIMS

- Revisit the key ingredients of narrative text.
- Analyse the structure of narrative text.

In this section you will build on your existing knowledge of how a narrative text works, thinking about its audience, purpose and form, and focusing on its typical structure and language features.

Audience, purpose, form

Narrative texts tell you an imaginary story. Some typical examples are:

- **novels**, like the *Harry Potter* series
- **traditional tales**, like *Cinderella.*

TYPICAL FEATURES

The typical features of narrative texts are listed below. You will need to refer to these in Section 2.

- The **audience** is someone who wants to be entertained and absorbed by a story.
- The **purpose** is to tell that story in an entertaining and interesting way.
- The **form** or structure of narrative often includes an opening (introduction), a series of events (the developing plot and complication), a crisis, and a resolution. The events are narrated in chronological order with a distinct narrative perspective (how the story is told) and longer stories are ordered into chapters.

Typical **language features** of narrative texts are:

- past tense, e.g. 'he said'
- first or third person, e.g. 'I' or 'he'
- powerful vocabulary helping to create just the picture the writer wants, e.g. 'roared'
- figurative language – powerful comparisons that help the reader picture what is being described, e.g. 'roared like a lion'
- dialogue to give the reader understanding of characters/to further plot, e.g. 'Can you tell me...'

Task 1 Reading and annotating

There are hundreds of ways to tell a story, but most have a beginning, a middle and an end. The first half of the story below has been annotated to show the language features listed on page 6. Annotate the second half to provide more examples of as many of the features as you can, including a brief note of the effect they have.

Time connectives (highlighted in mauve) – help the reader follow the chronology of the story

Chronological order – helps the reader understand how one event follows another

Dialogue – furthers plot and gives insight into character

How Long Will It Take?

One day Nasreddin Hodja was chopping wood close to the road a few kilometres from Akshehir. **After a while** a man came along the road, walking toward Akshehir, and he called to the Hodja,

'Can you tell me how long it will take me to get to Akshehir?'

The Hodja heard him and looked up from his work, but **he said** nothing. So the man called again, louder **this time**,

'How long will it take me to get to Akshehir?'

Still the Hodja said nothing, and this time the man **roared like a lion**,

'How long will it take me to get to Akshehir?'

When the Hodja did not answer even then, the man decided he must be deaf, and so he started walking rapidly toward the city. Nasreddin Hodja watched him for a moment, and then he shouted,

'It will take you about an hour!'

'Well, why didn't you say so before?' demanded the man angrily.

'First I had to know how fast you were going to walk,' answered the Hodja.

Traditional tale

Third-person narrative — story told by omniscient (all-knowing) author

Past tense

Powerful vocabulary and figurative language – help the reader picture what is being described

Time connectives

Task 2 Discussing

All the time connectives in the first part of the story have been highlighted in mauve. Connectives link the parts of sentences together. They indicate things like addition (e.g. 'also', 'furthermore'), opposition (e.g. 'on the one hand', 'however') and time (e.g. 'at first', 'in the end').

Identify all the time connectives in the remaining paragraphs of the extract. What difference would it make to the story if all the time connectives were deleted? Be prepared to present your ideas to the class.

The Art of Narrative Writing

Using text skeletons

In order to understand the structure of a text, it can be useful to draw a diagram or 'text skeleton'. Text skeletons represent the bare bones of a text.

A typical narrative skeleton resembles a timeline, but remember there are many different ways to structure a story so this type of skeleton only fits the 'typical' story structure.

The lines cutting across the timeline indicate significant stages in the story. The typical story has five stages, as shown below. The notes attached to each stage are memory joggers summing up the key events.

Using text skeletons will help you to analyse the structure of a text and plan your own writing.

Task 3 | **Structuring**

Below is a partially-completed text skeleton and memory joggers for *How Long Will It Take?* Complete the text skeleton and memory joggers for stages 4 and 5 so that you have a full set of notes on the text and a clear picture of its structure.

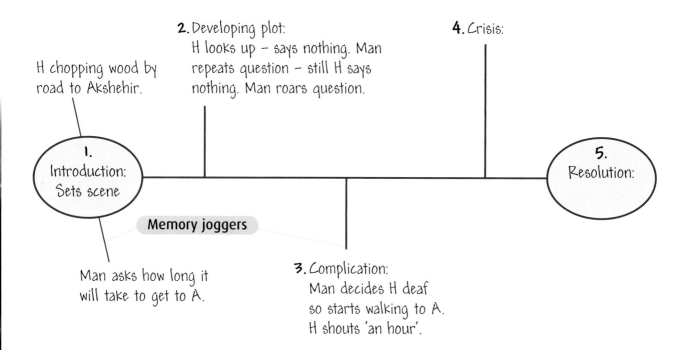

2. Developing plot:
H looks up – says nothing. Man repeats question – still H says nothing. Man roars question.

4. Crisis:

H chopping wood by road to Akshehir.

1. Introduction: Sets scene

5. Resolution:

Memory joggers

Man asks how long it will take to get to A.

3. Complication:
Man decides H deaf so starts walking to A. H shouts 'an hour'.

Learning from example

AIMS

- Reinforce the key ingredients of narrative text.
- Identify how storywriters compose their writing to suit audience and purpose and use narrative devices to involve the reader.
- Think about what sort of words make writing more effective.

In this section you will focus on a short story, and consider how the writer has tried to engage the reader's interest by the way she has composed her story.

Test watch As well as building up your writing skills, the following sections are good preparation for the optional reading tests at the end of Year 7 because they help you to:

- comment on a writer's purpose and the effects of the text on the reader
- comment on the structure and organisation of texts
- comment on a writer's use of language
- deduce, infer or interpret information, events or ideas
- describe, select or retrieve information, events or ideas from texts.

If you show these skills in the reading test, you will gain a better mark.

Task 4 ## Reading

 Charles, by Shirley Jackson, tells the story of a small boy starting nursery school. However, this event becomes a more significant milestone than his mother had expected.

As you read, consider:
- what makes the story entertaining
- how the writer ends the story.

(Note: Time connectives have been highlighted in mauve to help you follow the story, and see page 13 for a glossary of the more difficult words.)

Chronological order – helps the reader understand how one event follows another

Past tense

First-person narrative perspective (autobiographical style) – the writer tells the story as if it had happened to her

Charles

The day Laurie **started** kindergarten[1] he renounced corduroy overalls with bibs and began wearing blue jeans with a belt; **I** watched him go off the first morning with the older girl next door, seeing clearly that an era of my life was ended, my sweet-voiced nursery-school tot replaced by a long-trousered, **swaggering** character who forgot to stop at the corner and wave goodbye to me.

Powerful vocabulary – helps the reader picture what is being described

He came home the same way, the front door **slamming** open, his cap on the floor, and the voice suddenly became raucous shouting,

'Isn't anybody here?'

5

Time connectives – help the reader follow chronology of story

At lunch he spoke insolently to his father, spilled Jannie's milk, and remarked that his teacher said that we were not to take the name of the Lord in vain.

'How was school today?' I asked, elaborately casual.

'All right,' he said.

'Did you learn anything?' his father asked.

Dialogue – furthers plot and gives insight into character

Laurie regarded his father coldly. **'I didn't learn nothing,'** he said.

'Anything,' I said. 'Didn't learn anything.'

'The teacher spanked a boy, though,' Laurie said, addressing his bread and butter. 'For being fresh[2],' he added with his mouth full.

'What did he do?' I asked. 'Who was it?'

Laurie thought. 'It was Charles,' he said. 'He was fresh. The teacher spanked him and made him stand in a corner. He was awfully fresh.'

'What did he do?' I asked again, but Laurie slid off his chair, took a cookie, and left, while his father was still saying, 'See here, young man.'

The next day Laurie remarked at lunch, as soon as he sat down, 'Well, Charles was bad again today.' He grinned enormously and said, 'Today Charles hit the teacher.'

'Good heavens,' I said, mindful of the Lord's name, 'I suppose he got spanked again?'

'He sure did,' Laurie said. 'Look up,' he said to his father.

'What?' his father said, looking up.

'Look down,' Laurie said. 'Look at my thumb. Gee, you're dumb.' He began to laugh insanely.

'Why did Charles hit the teacher?' I asked quickly.

'Because she tried to make him colour with red crayons,' Laurie said. 'Charles wanted to colour with green crayons so he hit the teacher and she spanked him and said nobody play with Charles but everybody did.'

The third day – it was Wednesday of the first week – Charles bounced a seesaw onto the head of a little girl and made her bleed and the teacher made him stay inside all during recess.[3] **Thursday** Charles had to stand in a corner during story time because he kept pounding his feet on the floor. **Friday** Charles was deprived of blackboard privileges because he threw chalk.

On Saturday I remarked to my husband, 'Do you think kindergarten is too unsettling for Laurie? All this toughness and bad grammar, and this Charles boy sounds like such a bad influence.'

'It'll be all right,' my husband said reassuringly. 'Bound to be people like Charles in the world. Might as well meet them now as later.'

On Monday Laurie came home late, full of news. 'Charles,' he shouted as he came up the hill; I was waiting anxiously on the front steps, 'Charles,' Laurie yelled all the way up the hill, 'Charles was bad again.'

'Come right in,' I said, as soon as he came close enough. 'Lunch is waiting.'

'You know what Charles did?' he demanded, following me through the door. 'Charles yelled so in school they sent a boy in from first grade to tell the teacher she had to make Charles keep quiet, and so Charles had to stay after school. And so all the children stayed to watch him.' 55

'What did he do?' I asked.

'He just sat there,' Laurie said, climbing into his chair at the table. 'Hi Pop, y'old dust mop.' 60

'Charles had to stay after school today,' I told my husband. 'Everyone stayed with him.'

'What does this Charles look like?' my husband asked Laurie. 'What's his other name?'

'He's bigger than me,' Laurie said. 'And he doesn't have any rubbers[4] and he doesn't ever wear a jacket.' 65

Monday night was the first Parent-Teachers meeting, and only the fact that Jannie had a cold kept me from going; I wanted passionately to meet Charles's mother. **On Tuesday** Laurie remarked suddenly. 'Our teacher had a friend come see her in school today.' 70

'Charles's mother?' my husband and I asked simultaneously.

'Naaah,' Laurie said scornfully. 'It was a man who came and made us do exercises. Look.' He climbed down from his chair and squatted down and touched his toes. 'Like this,' he said. He got solemnly back into his chair and said, picking up his fork, Charles didn't even do exercises.' 75

'That's fine,' I said heartily. 'Didn't Charles want to do exercises?'

'Naaah,' Laurie said. 'Charles was so fresh to the teacher's friend he wasn't let do exercises.'

'Fresh again?' I said.

'He kicked the teacher's friend,' Laurie said. 'The teacher's friend told Charles to touch his toes like I just did and Charles kicked him.' 80

'What are they going to do about Charles, do you suppose?' Laurie's father asked him.

Laurie shrugged elaborately. 'Throw him out of the school, I guess,' he said. 85

Wednesday and Thursday were routine: Charles yelled during story hour and hit a boy in the stomach and made him cry. On Friday Charles stayed after school again and so did all the other children. With the third week of kindergarten Charles was an institution in our family: Jannie was being a Charles when she cried all afternoon; Laurie did a Charles when he filled his wagon full of mud and pulled it through the kitchen; even my husband, when he caught his elbow in the telephone cord and pulled telephone, ashtray, and a bowl of flowers off the table, said, after the first minute, 'Looks like Charles'. 90

During the third and fourth weeks there seemed to be a reformation in Charles; Laurie reported grimly at lunch on Thursday of the third week, Charles was so good today the teacher gave him an apple.'

'What?' I said, and my husband added warily, 'you mean Charles?'

'Charles,' Laurie said. 'He gave the crayons around and he picked up the books afterward and the teacher said he was her helper.'

'What happened?' I asked incredulously.

'He was her helper, that's all,' Laurie said, and shrugged.

'Can this be true, about Charles?' I asked my husband that night. 'Can something like this happen?'

'Wait and see,' my husband said cynically. 'When you've got a Charles to deal with, this may mean he's only plotting.'

He seemed to be wrong. For over a week Charles was the teacher's helper; each day he handed things out and he picked things up; no one had to stay after school.

'**The PTA meeting's next week again**,' I told my husband one evening. 'I'm going to find Charles's mother there.'

'Ask her what happened to Charles,' my husband said. 'I'd like to know.'

'I'd like to know myself,' I said.

On Friday of that week things were back to normal; 'you know what Charles did today?' Laurie demanded at the lunch table, in a voice slightly awed. 'He told a little girl to say a word and she said it and the teacher washed her mouth out with soap and Charles laughed.'

'What word?' his father asked unwisely, and Laurie said, 'I'll have to whisper it to you, it's so bad.' He got down off his chair and went around to his father. His father bent his head down and Laurie whispered joyfully. His father's eyes widened.

'Did Charles tell the little girl to say that?' he asked respectfully.

'She said it twice,' Laurie said. 'Charles told her to say it twice.'

'What happened to Charles?' my husband asked.

'Nothing,' Laurie said. 'He was passing out the crayons.'

Monday morning Charles abandoned the little girl and said the evil word himself three or four times, getting his mouth washed out with soap each time. He also threw chalk.

My husband came to the door with me **that evening** as I set out for the PTA meeting. 'Invite her over for a cup of tea after the meeting,' he said. 'I want to get a look at her.'

'If only she's there,' I said prayerfully.

'She'll be there,' my husband said. 'I don't see how they could hold a PTA[5] meeting without Charles's mother.'

At the meeting I sat restlessly, scanning each comfortable matronly face, trying to determine which one hid the secret of Charles. None of them looked to me haggard enough. No one stood up in the meeting and apologized for the way her son had been acting. No one mentioned Charles.

After the meeting I identified and sought out Laurie's kindergarten teacher. She had a plate with a cup of tea and a piece of chocolate cake; I had a plate with a cup of tea and a piece of marshmallow cake. We maneuvred up to one another cautiously and smiled.

'I've been so anxious to meet you,' I said. 'I'm Laurie's mother.'

'We're all so interested in Laurie,' she said.

'Well, he certainly likes kindergarten,' I said. 'He talks about it all the time.'

'We had a little trouble adjusting, the first week or so,' she said primly, 'but now he's a fine little helper. With lapses, of course.'

'Laurie usually adjusts very quickly,' I said. 'I suppose this time it's Charles's influence.'

'Charles?'

'Yes,' I said, laughing, 'you must have your hands full in that kindergarten, with Charles.'

'Charles?' she said. 'We don't have any Charles in the kindergarten.'

¹ **kindergarten** – nursery
² **fresh** – cheeky
³ **recess** – breaktime
⁴ **rubbers** – nappies
⁵ **PTA** – Parent-Teacher Association

Audience and purpose

Task 5 **Discussing**

 Every writer has to start by thinking about audience and purpose. Discuss who and what you think the audience and purpose of this extract is.

Features of narrative text

Writing a good story, like baking a good cake, depends on selecting the right ingredients and combining them effectively. The opening of this story (pages 9 and 10) has been annotated to bring out some key features of narrative text.

Task 6 **Annotating**

 Annotate the next section of the story (from line 17 up to line 33 'He began to laugh insanely') to illustrate one more example of these features and their effects.

Beginning the story effectively

Discussing

 Now look at the opening of *Charles* and reread the first 12 lines. Discuss the following:

- Why is the opening of any piece of writing the most important part?
- What features make the opening of *Charles* effective? Look at the list in the table below. Only some are relevant to *Charles*. Decide which ones apply and jot down evidence (using summary or brief quotation) to support your selection.

Ingredients for effective openings	Evidence to support selection
1. hook to grab reader's interest	
2. action	
3. shock tactics	
4. tension	
5. mystery	
6. interesting characterisation	
7. convincing dialogue	
8. good choice of words	
9. interesting sentence structure	
10. striking imagery	
11. effective description	

- In the opening lines, what hints are there about the way the story is going to develop? Be prepared to share your ideas.

Choosing powerful words

Descriptive writing is a common feature of many types of text. It is often thought of as a term that refers to narrative and recount writing rather than text like information or explanation. In fact, selecting the right words to describe something powerfully is a central ingredient of most forms of writing.

Discussing

 Reread the opening paragraph of *Charles*. The writer has selected her vocabulary very carefully to describe Laurie's appearance and attitude. Which words do you think are particularly effective?

The Art of Narrative Writing

Now look at the two versions of one paragraph from the story below – the differences have been highlighted in white. Discuss which one is the more effective. Be prepared to give reasons for your decision.

Original version

The third day – it was Wednesday of the first week – Charles bounced a seesaw onto the head of a little girl and made her bleed and the teacher made him stay inside all during recess. Thursday Charles had to stand in a corner during story time because he kept pounding his feet on the floor. Friday Charles was deprived of blackboard privileges because he threw chalk.

Adapted version

The third day – it was Wednesday of the first week – Charles hit a little girl on the head with a seesaw and made her bleed and the teacher made him stay inside all during recess. Thursday Charles had to stand in a comer during story time because he was hitting his feet on the floor. Friday Charles was not allowed to use the blackboard because he threw chalk.

Task 9 | **Discussing**

Scenario: A four-year-old girl/boy has taken an instant dislike to nursery school and has spent much of the first day crying. Brainstorm the best words to describe the following:

Be prepared to share the best of your ideas with the class.

3 Text structure and organisation

Getting the structure right

AIMS

- Analyse how the writer structured the information to match her intentions.

- Use an appropriate skeleton to note down key events.

- See how time connectives help link text chronologically and coherently.

In this section you will use a text skeleton to help analyse the structure of the story and think about what helps the text hang together.

Structuring the story

Structuring writing clearly and signposting how one section relates to another helps the reader to understand the text. Clear signposting is needed within paragraphs to help the reader follow how ideas are grouped, connected or developed. Using these techniques makes a text cohesive (see the explanation on page 56).

Task 10 Analysing and discussing

 Look at the completed text skeleton for *Charles* and talk about how the author has adapted the typical storytelling pattern to suit her purpose.

2. Developing plot:
Parents believe L's growing rudeness is because of bad influence of Charles – main figure in L's tales of school. C becomes household term for bad behaviour. L says C improved – has become teacher's helper.

4. Crisis:
Narrator speaks to L's teacher. Says L had problems settling but now a little helper. Asks about C. Discovers no one in nursery called Charles.

I. Introduction:
Mother (narrator) tells how proudly watched son (Laurie) go off for first day at nursery school – first stage in growing up. Left swaggering – returned rude and swaggering.

3. Complication:
Narrator can't wait to meet C's mother at PTA meeting but can't see anyone tired/weary enough. No one mentions C.

Note how the writer has chosen to end the story at the crisis point. She could, however, have chosen at least two alternatives to provide a resolution to her story:

- Ending with a short final paragraph telling us what Laurie's mother said/did/felt when she realised her son was 'Charles'.

- Ending with several paragraph telling us in detail what Laurie's mother said/did/felt when she realised her son was 'Charles'.

The Art of Narrative Writing

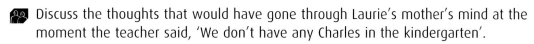 Discuss the thoughts that would have gone through Laurie's mother's mind at the moment the teacher said, 'We don't have any Charles in the kindergarten'.

Why do you think the author chose to end her story with the teacher's words? Is this an effective way to end the story? Be prepared to present your ideas.

> Of course there's a Charles... Oh no!

Using time connectives to guide the reader

Guiding the reader clearly through key events is important. Narrative text often relies on time connectives acting as signposts to help the reader know where they are in the story.

Task 11 | Analysing

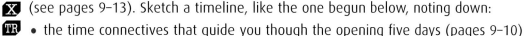 The time connectives throughout the story have been highlighted in mauve (see pages 9–13). Sketch a timeline, like the one begun below, noting down:

- the time connectives that guide you though the opening five days (pages 9–10)
- the key events
- how many lines the writer has used to cover each day.

Note: The first two days have been completed for you.

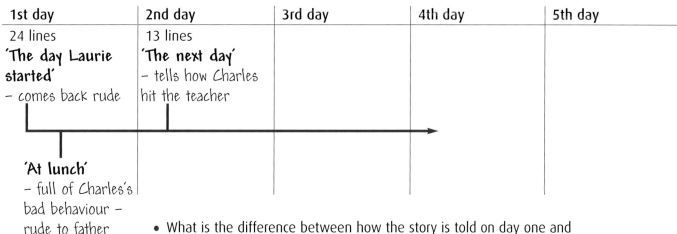

1st day	2nd day	3rd day	4th day	5th day
24 lines 'The day Laurie started' – comes back rude	13 lines 'The next day' – tells how Charles hit the teacher			

'At lunch' – full of Charles's bad behaviour – rude to father

- What is the difference between how the story is told on day one and how it is told on days three to five? Be prepared to present your answers.
- Why do you think the writer gave so many lines to the first day and so few for the last three days of the week?

Task 12 | Planning practice

Brainstorm things that could happen to students in their first few weeks at secondary school. Discuss which idea to focus on.

Then use a narrative text skeleton to plan the outline for the story. For example, decide if your story will include a resolution or end at the crisis point like *Charles*.

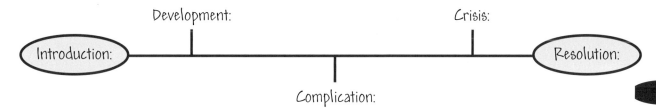

Development:

Crisis:

Introduction:

Resolution:

Complication:

Sentence structure and punctuation

Making the sentences work

AIMS

- Discuss the difference varying sentence structure makes to the quality of writing.

- Write and redraft a scene focusing on sentence variety including complex sentences.

- Give advice on how to use dialogue to help tell a story.

In this section you will develop your ability to improve your writing by varying the sentence structures you use. You will focus on sentence variety and selecting powerful vocabulary.

Varying the structure of sentences

Task 13 **Analysing**

Read the extract from *Charles* below. The colour-coding indicates different types of sentences. Remember that connectives are in mauve.

> At the meeting, I sat restlessly, scanning each comfortable matronly face, trying to determine which one hid the secret of Charles. None of them looked to me haggard enough. No one stood up in the meeting and apologized for the way her son had been acting. No one mentioned Charles.
>
> After the meeting, I identified and sought out Laurie's kindergarten teacher. She had a plate with a cup of tea and a piece of chocolate cake; I had a plate with a cup of tea and a piece of marshmallow cake. We maneuvred up to one another cautiously and smiled.

GRAMMAR

Clauses

A **main clause** is a single idea or event – it has a subject and one verb and makes complete sense on its own.

A **simple sentence** has one main clause.

A **compound sentence** is two or more simple sentences (main clauses) joined together with coordinating conjunctions (e.g. 'and', 'but', 'so', 'or').

A **complex sentence** is one main clause plus at least one subordinate clause. A subordinate clause doesn't make complete sense on its own – it relies on the main clause to make sense.

- Which colour represents which sentence type? Be prepared to present your ideas.
- Each green sentence is made up of two main clauses joined together. Which coordinating conjunction joins the clauses together in most of these sentences?
- What would you have to do to change the final green sentence into two yellow-type sentences?
- What is the difference between simple sentences and compound sentences?
- If you wanted to change the last sentence into a blue-type sentence, what could you do? Try beginning the sentence with one of these words: Cautiously.../ Manoeuvring.../After...
- Look at this sentence:

  She had a plate with a cup of tea and a piece of chocolate cake; I had a plate with a cup of tea and a piece of marshmallow cake.

- Why do you think the writer chose to make what could be two sentences into one with a semicolon?
- Which colours have been used to highlight time connectives and conjunctions? Be prepared to present your responses.

Writing effective dialogue

One problem with telling a story that relies on speech is that the amount of speech can get out of hand and become boring. On the other hand, well-written dialogue can really move the story along and help the reader to picture the characters.

Task 14 **Analysing**

 Look at this short extract and compare it with the adapted extract on page 20, which has summed up the events without using dialogue. Decide which version is more effective, giving reasons for your decision. Consider what helps the scene come alive and what difference the actual speech makes to your picture of Charles.

Original extract

On Monday Laurie came home late, full of news. 'Charles,' he shouted as he came up the hill; I was waiting anxiously on the front steps, 'Charles,' Laurie yelled all the way up the hill, 'Charles was bad again.'

'Come right in,' I said, as soon as he came close enough. 'Lunch is waiting.'

'You know what Charles did?' he demanded, following me through the door.

'Charles yelled so in school they sent a boy in from first grade to tell the teacher she had to make Charles keep quiet, and so Charles had to stay after school. And so all the children stayed to watch him.'

Adapted extract

On Monday Laurie came home late, full of news and repeatedly yelling Charles's name as he came up the hill; I was waiting anxiously on the front steps and he told me that Charles had been bad again. I welcomed him in and, when he came close enough, informed him that lunch was ready. He followed me through the door, demanding that I guess what Charles had done today. He told me that Charles had yelled so much in school that a boy had been sent in from first grade to tell the teacher to make Charles keep quiet. Consequently, Charles had been in detention after school. All the children stayed to watch him.

Task 15 ## Advising

Discuss how you would reorder the advice below on how to lay out and punctuate speech so that the most important points come first. Link your advice to the colour-coding used on the extract on page 19.

Then decide how you would use this extract and the advice to explain to a nine-year-old child how to lay out and punctuate direct speech properly. Be prepared to present your advice to the class.

Advice

Commas: Use a comma to separate what is said from who says it, unless there is a '?' or '!'. Always put the comma (or other punctuation) immediately in front of the speech marks.

Capital letter: Begin direct speech with a capital letter.

Speech marks: Put speech marks ('') round the direct speech.

Paragraphs: Begin a new paragraph for each new speaker.

5 · Composing your own story

AIMS

- Write a short story focusing on composing it effectively.
- Plan, draft and revise the story with reader and purpose in mind.
- Plan your narrative perspective and use a range of narrative devices to involve the reader.
- Portray character effectively through descriptive dialogue and action.

Your task

Plan and write a story called *The First Day*. You will use what you have learned about how *Charles* was written to help make your story entertaining and hold the interest of your readers.

Test watch This writing task is good preparation for the type of writing required in your English tests because it helps you learn how to:

plan your work so that it is organised logically into well-constructed paragraphs that are linked together well

compose your writing effectively to match its audience and purpose,

and select powerful vocabulary

vary the structure of your sentences and punctuate them correctly.

If you show these skills in the optional English test at the end of Year 7, you will gain a better mark.

1 Improvising the content

A child is starting nursery or secondary school. His/her parents are concerned that she/he either won't fit in or will be bullied by rough children.

You have five minutes to plan your improvisation of an incident that happens on the first day. Be prepared to present your scenario.

2 Planning the structure

Structuring and organising your ideas is the most important aspect of effective writing. Text skeletons are very useful tools to help you do this.

Using the improvisations you have just seen, sketch a narrative skeleton to help you plan your story outline, adapting it as necessary.

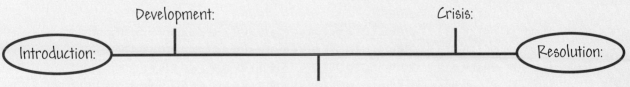

Development:

Crisis:

Introduction:

Resolution:

Complication:

The Art of Narrative Writing

Composing your piece

 Now you are ready to start writing.

Points to remember

As you write, remember to:

- make the opening grab your reader's interest by trying to picture someone who will be reading your story as you write (see page 14)
- use time connectives to make the story easy to follow (see pages 7 and 17)
- select powerful vocabulary that will help the reader picture the scene (see page 14)

- select the right amount of speech to help tell your story and give insight into the characters without becoming boring (see page 19)
- check that the speech is correctly paragraphed and punctuated (see page 20)
- vary the length of sentences and construct them to create just the picture you want (see page 18)
- make the ending effective (see pages 16 and 17).

You may want to use some of the sentence signposts and connectives below to help you.

> **Sentence signposts and connectives**
> - The day I started nursery school (first person – child's viewpoint)
> - The day X started nursery school, I (first person – another person's viewpoint)
> - The day X started nursery school, his mother (third person – not personally involved)
> - Secondary school was going to be different
> - Everything was fine until first break
> - As soon as the final bell began to ring
> - By lunchtime,
> - On the way home from school

 ## Peer comment

Swap your draft with your partner's and read each other's carefully. Discuss what works well and highlight this on the drafts. Then discuss how you could improve particular sections. Jot down your suggestions on the draft.

Redraft your writing where necessary, using your partner's comments to guide you.

Pulling it all together

 Listen to extracts from stories written by members of your class.

Decide what are the key features that make these extracts effective.

Be prepared to feed your ideas back to the class.

Set up to three targets for yourself for improving your next piece of narrative writing.

B The Art of Recount Writing

 **How recount text works**

AIMS

- Revisit the key ingredients of recount text,
- Analyse the structure of recount text.

In this section you will build on your existing knowledge of how a recount text works, thinking about its audience, purpose and form, and focusing on its typical structure and language features.

Audience, purpose, form

Recount texts tell you the story of events and experiences that have actually happened. Some typical examples are:

- **autobiographies** in which someone tells their own life story
- **biographies** in which someone tells someone else's life story
- **newspaper articles** about an incident.

TYPICAL FEATURES

The typical features of recount texts are listed below. You will need to refer to these in Section 2.

- The **audience** is someone who is interested in what happened.
- The **purpose** is to tell the reader what happened in an informative and entertaining way.
- The **form** or structure of recount text often includes paragraphs in chronological order, time connectives, and topic sentences.

Typical **language features** of recount texts are:

- past tense, e.g. 'improved'
- first or third person, e.g. 'people' (third)
- time connectives , e.g. 'Throughout the ages'
- personal or impersonal, depending on purpose, e.g. 'in the middle of the 17th century, accuracy improved incredibly' (impersonal)
- vocabulary to help to create the picture the writer wants, e.g. 'more precisely' and 'earliest mechanical clocks'
- figurative language (imagery) – powerful comparisons that help the reader picture what is being described, e.g. 'It resembled a tiny earth'

The typical features of narrative and recount texts are similar in that both tell a story. The key difference is purpose, since a recount text should be fact not fiction.

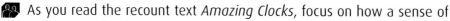

Task 1   Reading and annotating

As you read the recount text *Amazing Clocks*, focus on how a sense of chronological order is maintained. Annotate the second half of the text to illustrate another example of each annotated feature.

Time connectives – emphasise chronological order

Paragraphs – organised in chronological order

Impersonal and formal language – to focus on the events

Third person

Powerful vocabulary – to help the reader picture what is described

Past tense – to recount events that have happened

Amazing Clocks

Throughout the ages, **people** have tried to measure time more and more **precisely.**

The earliest mechanical clocks of the 14th century were accurate to about 20 minutes per day. **With the invention of the pendulum clock in the middle of the 17th century, accuracy improved incredibly,** to plus or minus ten seconds per day.

Until the 19th century, people who owned watches had to check the accurate time by comparing the watch with a sundial. With new technology in the 1930s, quartz crystal clocks were able to keep time to about to about two milliseconds per day.

Today, the world's best timekeeper is the 'caesium atomic fountain' clock, which is accurate to one second in 15 million years.

Given that standard recount text is in the past tense, why do you think the last paragraph is in the present tense? Be prepared to present your ideas.

Task 2   Discussing

All the time connectives in the extract have been highlighted in mauve. Discuss the function these words and phrases have in the recount. Be prepared to present your ideas.

Using text skeletons to help you

In order to understand the structure of a text, it can be useful to draw a diagram or 'text skeleton'. Text skeletons represent the bare bones of a text.

The typical recount skeleton resembles a timeline. The lines cutting across the timeline indicate significant stages in the recount. The notes attached to each stage are memory joggers summing up the key events, for example: '14C – Earliest mechanical clocks – Accurate to 20 mins per day'.

Using text skeletons will help you both to analyse the structure of a text and to plan your own writing.

Task 3   Structuring

Below is a partially-completed text skeleton for *Amazing Clocks*. Complete the memory joggers so that you have a full set of notes on the text.

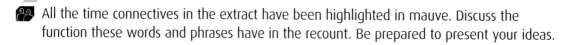

1. 14C – Earliest mechanical clocks – accurate to 20 mins per day

2. Mid-17C – pendulum clock invented – accurate to +/– 10 secs

3. Until 19C had to compare watch with sundial for accuracy

4.

5.

Memory jogger

Once you have completed the skeleton, mark where the writer has chosen to put the paragraph breaks with the symbol // . Why do you think the writer chose to start new paragraphs at these points?

Learning from example

AIMS

- Revisit the key ingredients of recount text.

- Identify how writers adapt their writing to suit audience and purpose and involve the reader.

- Comment on how writers use imagery to engage reader's interest and link ideas.

In this section you will focus on the beginning of a recount text and think about what techniques the writer has used to try to engage the reader's interest.

Test watch As well as building up your writing skills, the following sections are good preparation for the optional reading tests at the end of Year 7 because they help you to:

- comment on a writer's purpose and the effects of the text on the reader

- comment on the structure and organisation of texts

- comment on a writer's use of language

- deduce, infer or interpret information, events or ideas

- describe, select or retrieve information, events or ideas from texts.

If you show these skills in the reading test, you will gain a better mark.

Audience and purpose

Task 4 **Reading and discussing**

 The extract on page 26 gives the opening paragraphs of *Longitude* by Dava Sobel – the dramatic story of the race to work out how sailors could accurately plot their position at sea. It tells the reader how one man, John Harrison, devoted 40 years of his life to creating the perfect timekeeper to solve the longitude problem and win the fortune offered to the first person to do so. As you read the passage, consider:

- why might Dava Sobel have chosen to begin this biography of John Harrison in such an autobiographical way, with her own early memory of thinking about longitude?

- what imagery has she chosen? Find at least two examples that strike you.

- who and what do you think are the audience and purpose of this extract?

Time connectives – emphasise chronological order

Topic sentence – introduces central focus of passage

First person – because this part of the recount is autobiographical

Past tense – recounts past events

Powerful vocabulary and comparison – helps reader picture what is being described

Paragraphs – organised in chronological order

Formal language – suits purpose of text

Once on a Wednesday excursion when **I was** a little girl, my father bought me a beaded wire ball that I loved. At a touch, I could **collapse the toy into a flat coil** between my palms, or pop it open to make a hollow sphere. **Rounded out, it resembled a tiny Earth**, because its hinged wires traced the same pattern of intersecting circles that I had seen on the **globe in my schoolroom – the thin black lines of latitude and longitude**. The few coloured beads slid along the wire haphazardly, like ships on the high seas.

My father strode up Fifth Avenue to the Rockefeller Center with me on his shoulders, and we stopped to stare at the statue of Atlas, carrying Heaven and Earth on his.

The bronze orb that Atlas held aloft, like the wire toy in my hands, was a see-through world, defined by imaginary lines. The Equator. The Ecliptic. The Tropic of Cancer. The Tropic of Capricorn. The Arctic Circle. The prime meridian. Even then I could recognize, in the graph-paper grid imposed on the globe, a powerful symbol of all the real lands and waters on the planet.

Today, the latitude and longitude lines govern with more authority than I could have imagined forty-odd years ago, for they stay fixed as the world changes its configuration underneath them – with continents adrift across a widening sea, and national boundaries repeatedly redrawn by war or peace.

Features of recount text

Task 5 **Annotating**

The first part of the extract above has been annotated to bring out some key language features of a recount text. Annotate the rest of the text to illustrate as many of these features as possible. Once you have identified the features, note down the effect they have.

Using imagery to engage the reader

Writers often use imagery to grab the reader's interest and sometimes help the reader link the ideas from one paragraph to another. For example, *Longitude* begins with the writer vividly describing the 'beaded wire ball that I loved'.

Discussing

 Ask one member of the group to read aloud the opening three paragraphs of *Longitude*. Discuss the use the writer makes of the image of the beaded wire ball to connect the three paragraphs and how effective this is. Jot down your findings under the following headings. Be prepared to present your conclusions.

Image of beaded ball	How it helps to link text and effect
Rounded out, it resembles a tiny Earth	Makes the reader picture the shape of the Earth and the child's amazement

Selecting the right level of formality

GRAMMAR

Standard English – the type of spoken and written English used when formal English is appropriate. Standard English is the language used by the majority of speakers of English

Task 7 **Analysing**

 Writers select how formal they want their writing to be. In the table below, four levels of formality are described and illustrated. Select the one you think best sums up the level of formality of the opening of *Longitude*, supported by evidence from the passage. Why do you think the writer chose this level of formality?

Level	Description	Example
1	**Informal** – largely written in colloquial language (slangy) English or dialect, resembling casual speech	'There was a feller here once by the name of Jim Smiley, in the winter of '49 – or maybe it was the spring of '50 – I don't recollect exactly;'
2	**Mixed** – some colloquial and some Standard English – often to bring out character through speech.	'We hide under the Akky Duck and arter that you can see 'em squintin' through the winders.' The veins about my heart tied themselves in knots...
3	**Formal but friendly** – Standard English used throughout but engages reader in a personal way through use of imagery and powerful words	In a place far different from where you are now grows an oak-tree by a lake. Round the oak's trunk is a chain of golden links. Tethered to the chain is a learned cat...
4	**Very formal** – Standard English used throughout. Impersonal and precise but unengaging language.	Interest will cease to be payable in respect of the cash within your Account on the day that...

The Art of Recount Writing

Getting the structure right

AIMS

- Analyse how the writer organised the information to match her intentions.

- Note down the key points of a text.

- Extend the range of words and phrases used to signpost texts.

- Recognise cues to start a new paragraph and use the first sentence to orientate the reader.

- See how time connectives help link the text chronologically.

In this section you will first analyse the structure of text using a text skeleton. Then you will explore how the text hangs together, focusing on how the ideas are grouped in paragraphs using connectives.

Structuring a recount

Structuring writing clearly and signposting how one section relates to another helps the reader to understand the text. Clear signposting is also needed within paragraphs to help the reader follow how ideas are grouped, connected or developed. Using these techniques makes a text cohesive (see the explanation on page 56).

Task 8 ▸ **Reading**

 Read this extract from *Longitude* carefully, where the writer includes some personal milestones (significant events) in Harrison's life. As you read, think about:

- how much of the passage is chronological
- at what point the passage stops being chronological.

(1) Forthright in his personal encounters, Harrison proposed marriage to Elizabeth Barrel, and she became his wife on August 30, 1718. Their son, John, was born the following summer. Then Elizabeth fell ill and died in the spring before the boy turned seven.

(2) The dearth[1] of detail regarding the widower's private life at this juncture[2] comes as no surprise, for he left no diaries or letters describing his activities or his angst.[3] Nevertheless, the parish records show that he found a new bride, ten years younger, within six months of Elizabeth's death. Harrison wed his second wife, Elizabeth Scott, on November 23, 1726. At the start of their 50 years together they had two children – William, born in 1728, who was to become his father's champion and right-hand man, and Elizabeth, born in 1732, about whom nothing is known save the date of her baptism, December 21. John, the child of Harrison's first marriage, died when he was only eighteen.

(3) No one knows when or how Harrison first heard word of the longitude prize. Some say that the nearby port of Hull, just five miles north of Harrison's home and the third largest port in England, would have been abuzz with news. From there, any seaman or merchant could have carried the announcement downstream across the Humber on the ferry.

(4) One would imagine that Harrison grew up well aware of the longitude problem – just as any alert schoolchild nowadays knows that cancer cries out for a cure and that there's no good way to get rid of nuclear waste. Longitude posed the greatest technological challenge of Harrison's age. He seems to have begun thinking of a way to tell time and longitude at sea even before Parliament promised any reward for doing so – or at least before he learned of the posted reward. In any case, whether his thoughts favoured longitude, Harrison kept busy with tasks that prepared to solve the problem.

¹ **dearth** – inadequate amount
² **juncture** – point in time
³ **angst** – sense of anxiety

Task 9 **Structuring**

   Look at the first two paragraphs on page 28, which recount some key personal events in Harrison's life. Complete a recount skeleton, using memory joggers to note the key events as far as the end of the second paragraph.

I. H married Eliz Barrett 1718

2. Son John born 1719

Now mark two lines (//) to indicate the paragraph break. Why do you think Dava Sobel chose to divide this information into two paragraphs?

Why do you think she chose to use phrases like 'the following summer' rather than giving every precise date?

Using topic sentences

A **topic sentence** (or key sentence) is the sentence in a paragraph that signposts the focus of the paragraph. The topic sentence is often the first sentence of the paragraph.

Task 10 **Discussing**

The account of some key points in Harrison's life on pages 28–29 has been divided into four paragraphs, with each topic sentence highlighted in orange.

 Discuss why the writer has ordered them in this way. Be prepared to feed back your ideas.

Using time connectives

The first two paragraphs retell specific events linked to particular dates. For this reason time connectives have been chosen to link the text. Four examples of these have been highlighted in mauve in the first two paragraphs.

Task 11 · Analysing

Look at paragraphs 1 and 2 on page 28. Could the writer have chosen to place all of the highlighted connecting phrases at the beginning of each sentence? Rephrase the first three sentences, so that they begin with the highlighted connective. For example: instead of 'Their son, John, was born the following summer', write **The following summer,** their son John was born.

Could the phrases have been placed anywhere else within their sentences? See if you can rephrase the first two sentences, again with the connective in another position. For example: John, their son, was born **the following summer**.

Time connectives are often placed at the beginning of a sentence. Why do you think the writer has avoided doing this? Be prepared to present your ideas.

Using sentence signposts to guide the reader

Paragraphs 3 and 4 of the extract do not recount definite events but reflect on how Harrison might have learned of the longitude prize and problem. Phrases indicating uncertainty have been used here instead of time connectives.

Task 12 · Analysing

Reread the last two paragraphs. Jot down any phrases that tell the reader that the writer is uncertain of the information given here.

> **Typical sentence signposts indicating uncertainty**
> It's hard to say   Possibly
> Apparently   It is thought
> It's not known when

Task 13 · Planning practice

Sketch a timeline, indicating the key things that have happened to you so far today. Next to each memory jogger, write the connective or beginning of the topic sentence that could introduce this section.

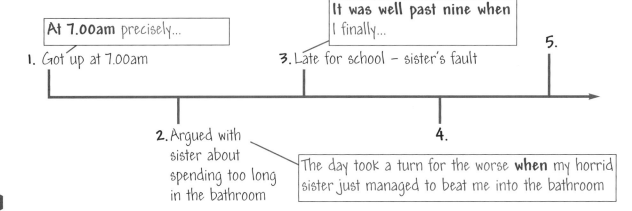

At 7.00am precisely...

It was well past nine when I finally...

1. Got up at 7.00am
2. Argued with sister about spending too long in the bathroom
3. Late for school – sister's fault

The day took a turn for the worse **when** my horrid sister just managed to beat me into the bathroom

4.

5.

Sentence structure and punctuation

Making the sentences work

AIMS

Explore the functions of subordinate clauses.

Look at how subordinate clauses can be used in different places within a sentence.

See how punctuation can make the meaning clear.

In this section you will learn more about complex sentences and look at how varying sentence structure helps engage the reader.

Varying the structure of sentences

Look at these two **simple sentences**.

1. Harrison lived near the sea. He was probably aware of the longitude problem.

Written like this, the connection between living near the sea and being aware of the longitude prize is not made clear. If you link the two sentences with a simple joining word like 'and' (thus making a **compound sentence**), the logical connection is still unclear.

2. Harrison lived near the sea and was probably aware of the longitude problem.

Complex sentences are useful because they help you link ideas effectively by bringing out the logical relationship between the events or ideas; they can also provide extra information about words or phrases.

3. Because he lived near the sea, Harrison was probably aware of the longitude problem.

> **GRAMMAR**
>
> A complex sentence includes a **main clause** (which makes sense all on its own and could therefore be a sentence) and at least one **subordinate clause**. Subordinate clauses do not make sense on their own but rely on a main clause to complete the sense. Commas mark the boundary between subordinate clauses and the main clauses to help the reader follow the sentences.

Subordinating conjunctions

> **GRAMMAR**
>
> Subordinate clauses often begin with a **subordinating conjunction** – a connective that makes a clear link with the main clause.
>
> - **when:** before, after, since, until
> - **where:** where, wherever
> - **on what condition:** although, if, when
> - **how:** by, as if
> - **why:** because, since, as
>
> 4. Since Harrison lived near the sea, he was probably aware of the longitude problem.

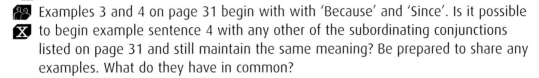

Task 14 **Structuring sentences**

Examples 3 and 4 on page 31 begin with with 'Because' and 'Since'. Is it possible to begin example sentence 4 with any other of the subordinating conjunctions listed on page 31 and still maintain the same meaning? Be prepared to share any examples. What do they have in common?

Using embedded clauses

Sometimes subordinate clauses are added into the middle of a clause to provide more information about whatever is being written. These are known as **embedded clauses** and often begin with 'who', 'whose', 'which' or 'that'.

5. Harrison, **who** lived near the sea, was probably aware of the longitude problem.

Task 15 **Structuring sentences**

Look at the two sentences below and redraft them so they have the same embedded clause pattern as example 5 above.

1 Having forgotten to set the alarm clock, Jo was late for school.

2 Feeling tired, the motorist decided to stop at the next services.

Begin your sentences like this:

1 Jo, who...   **2** The motorist,...

Spinning sentences

The structure of complex sentences provides you with a wide variety of ways to show the interrelationship between ideas or events. It is all a question of 'spinning' your sentences in a range of ways to engage your reader's interest.

6. Rounded out, it resembled a tiny Earth, because its hinged wires traced the same pattern of intersecting circles that I had seen in my schoolroom – the thin black lines of latitude and longitude.

Task 16 **Structuring sentences**

Example 6 consists of a main clause (underlined) and four subordinate clauses.

Discuss whether it is effective. Have reasons to back up your decision.

Rewrite each group of simple sentences below as one interesting, complex sentence.

1 Leon lived near the sea. He went swimming most days. He was a very good swimmer.

You might like to begin like this: Leon, who...

2 Julie was watching the television. She flicked from channel to channel. She was trying to find something interesting to watch.

3 Al had just woken up. He peered at the clock sleepily. He knew he was going to be late again.

AIMS

- Plan, draft and revise a recount text with reader and purpose in mind, maintaining the past tense and using temporal connectives to achieve clear chronology.

- Organise ideas into a coherent sequence of paragraphs using the first sentence to effectively orientate the reader and including supporting information within the paragraph.

- Vary your sentence structure to lend pace, variety and emphasis.

Your task

Write your own biographical account of an astronomer's life and achievements. Use what you have learned in this unit to hold the interest of your readers.

Test watch This writing task is good preparation for the type of writing required in your English tests because it helps you learn how to:

- plan your work so that it is organised logically into well-constructed paragraphs that are linked together well

- compose your writing effectively to match its audience and purpose,

- and select powerful vocabulary

- vary the structure of your sentences and punctuate them correctly.

If you show these skills in the optional English test at the end of Year 7, you will gain a better mark.

1 Audience and purpose

 Your task is to write an interesting account of the life and achievements of Afghan astronomer Ulug'bek, with the title 'Ulug'bek and the Conquest of the Stars'. Your audience is young people or adults who are interested in the stars.

- Discuss what effect the audience and purpose of this recount will have on the style. In particular consider these questions:

  - Will the recount be informal, formal or a mixture of the two?

  - How will you help the reader follow the information?

2 Structuring the content

 Read this list of key milestones in the life of Ulug'bek. They have been jotted down at random from a Middle Eastern travel book.

The Art of Recount Writing

built observatory in Samarkand in 1428 – the best equipped anywhere in the medieval world	1437: made a star catalogue giving very accurate positions of 992 stars
29 October 1449: assassinated because his findings conflicted with religious beliefs	unknown in West until a copy of his star catalogue discovered in Oxford's Bodleian Library in 1648
observatory destroyed by religious fanatics shortly after his beheading	significance of Ulug'bek's work largely ignored in the West
interest in astronomy inspired by his teacher Kazi Zade Rumi, whose motto was 'Where knowledge starts, religion ends.'	twentieth-century memorial is inscribed with his comment that infuriated his religious opponents: 'Religion disperses like a fog, kingdoms perish but the works of scholars remain for an eternity.'
one astronomer escaped with a copy of the star catalogue	1908: a Russian amateur archaeologist unearthed a giant sextant on the edge of Samarkand – one of the major finds of the twentieth century
grandson of the great conqueror Tamburlaine	
born in Afghanistan in 1394	

3 Planning the structure

It is important that you structure and organise your ideas before starting writing.

Organise the points in the list above chronologically as a recount skeleton.

Decide where you are going to place the information with no dates. You may be able to link them to information already on the skeleton, as in the 1394 box below.

Use a different colour to mark the paragraphs on your recount skeleton, using the // symbol. Write the topic of each paragraph next to each dividing line.

> 1394 born in Afghanistan
>
> ↓
>
> 1428 built observatory in Samarkand – best in world
>
> ↓
>
> 1437 made star catalogue

Top tip You will probably have to adjust your plan when you start writing the paragraphs.

Composing your piece

 Now you are ready to start writing.

Points to remember

As you write, remember to:

- begin in an effective way that will grab the reader's interest (see pages 25–26)
- select the appropriate level of formality for your audience and purpose (see page 27)
- paragraph your work using topic sentences to guide the reader (see page 29)
- link your ideas clearly using connectives appropriately and vary how you position these signposts within the sentences to avoid beginning every sentence with the date when the event happened (see page 30)

- try and make your sentences interesting. Think about how to spin clauses to make your complex sentences interesting. Use short simple sentences to add variety and focus (see pages 31–32).
- select powerful words to create the picture you want (see pages 26–27)
- end in a memorable way.

You may want to use some of the sentence signposts and connectives below to help you.

Sentence signposts and connectives
- was amazed to realise that anyone had
- Because his findings
- Shortly after
- In 1908
- Why is it that a man who accurately plotted the movement of the stars in 1437 is
- Over 450 years after
- Nine years later
- By the age of 34
- Ulug'bek, the grandson of

 # Peer comment

 Swap your draft with your partner's and read each other's carefully. Discuss what works well and highlight this on the drafts. Then discuss how you could improve particular sections. Jot down your suggestions on the draft.

- Redraft your writing where necessary, using your partner's comments to guide you.

 # Pulling it all together

- Listen to extracts from 'Ulug'bek and the Conquest of the Stars' written by members of your class.
- Decide what are the key features that make these extracts effective. Be prepared to feed your ideas back to the class.
- Set up to three targets for yourself for improving your next piece of recount writing.

C The Art of Information Writing

How information text works

AIMS

- Revisit the key ingredients of information text.
- Analyse the structure of information text.

In this section you will build on your existing knowledge of how an information text works, thinking about its audience, purpose and form.

Audience, purpose, form

Information texts tell us about the key characteristics of places, people, animals, concepts or things. Their purpose is to present information so that it is easy to find and understand. They often help the reader understand by drawing comparisons and pointing out what things have in common. Some typical examples of information texts are:

- **dictionaries**, such as *Collins Concise Dictionary*
- **reference books**, such as *Flowers of the Mediterranean*
- **text books**, such as *Geography of the United Kingdom*.

TYPICAL FEATURES

The typical features of information texts are listed below. You will need to refer to these in Section 2.

- The **audience** is someone who wants to know about something.
- The **purpose** is to present information so that it is easy to understand.
- The **form** or structure of information text often includes: an opening that introduces the topic, paragraphs in logical not chronological order, and topic sentences to introduce key points (usually the first sentence of a paragraph).

Typical **language features** of information texts are:

- formal language, which is sometimes impersonal, e.g. 'it seems impossible to move backwards in time'
- technical vocabulary, e.g. 'the cyclical, repetitive nature'
- present tense, e.g. 'Our senses tell us'
- generalisations summing up the key points, e.g. 'another aspect of time that we can perceive'
- detail, where necessary, to illustrate a point, e.g. 'such as the regular pattern of the seasons'.

Task 1 ## Reading and annotating

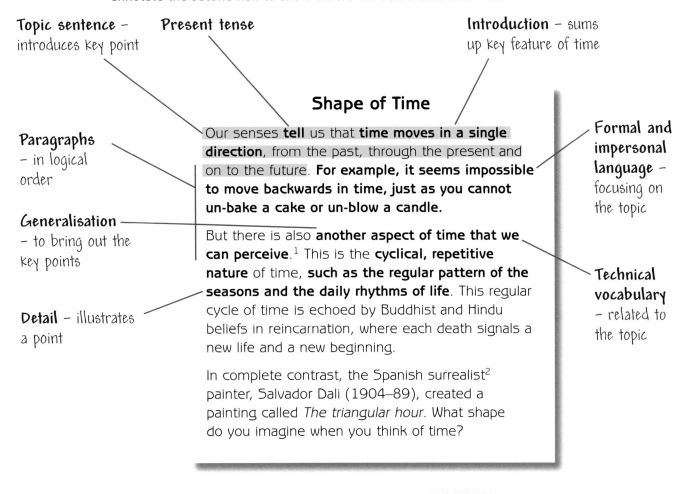

The start of the extract below has been annotated to illustrate all the language features of an information text. Read the extract and the annotations carefully, then annotate the second half to show where the same elements occur.

Topic sentence – introduces key point

Present tense

Introduction – sums up key feature of time

Shape of Time

Our senses **tell** us that **time moves in a single direction**, from the past, through the present and on to the future. **For example, it seems impossible to move backwards in time, just as you cannot un-bake a cake or un-blow a candle.**

But there is also **another aspect of time that we can perceive.**[1] This is the **cyclical, repetitive nature** of time, **such as the regular pattern of the seasons and the daily rhythms of life**. This regular cycle of time is echoed by Buddhist and Hindu beliefs in reincarnation, where each death signals a new life and a new beginning.

In complete contrast, the Spanish surrealist[2] painter, Salvador Dali (1904–89), created a painting called *The triangular hour*. What shape do you imagine when you think of time?

Paragraphs – in logical order

Generalisation – to bring out the key points

Detail – illustrates a point

Formal and impersonal language – focusing on the topic

Technical vocabulary – related to the topic

[1] **perceive** – be aware of

[2] **surrealist** – someone who follows surrealism, an artistic movement in the 1920s known for putting images from completely different contexts side by side to suggest unconscious or dreamlike states

Topic sentences

Look at the first sentence of the extract above, highlighted in orange. It is a topic sentence that introduces the topic of the paragraph. Most information writing uses topic sentences to guide the reader through the meaning of the text.

 Task 2 ## Discussing

Identify the two topic sentences in the remaining two paragraphs of the passage. Be prepared to share your conclusions.

Using text skeletons

In order to understand the structure of a text, it can be useful to draw a diagram or 'text skeleton'. Text skeletons represent the bare bones of a text.

A typical information skeleton is a spidergram. Each bubble around the subject in the centre represents a particular topic (often a single paragraph in the text). In the *Shape of Time* skeleton below, there are three paragraphs, so there are three bubbles connected to the subject bubble. The notes in each bubble tell the reader the topic of each paragraph. For example: '2. Cyclical repetitive nature' is a shortened version of the topic sentence that begins paragraph 2. The lines branching from each bubble are points connected to the main focus, for example 'Regular pattern of seasons'. These notes are called memory joggers.

Using text skeletons will help you to analyse the structure of a text and plan your own writing.

Task 3 **Structuring**

Below is a partially-completed text skeleton for *Shape of Time*. Discuss what point you would put in bubble 3. Decide what supporting memory joggers you would add.

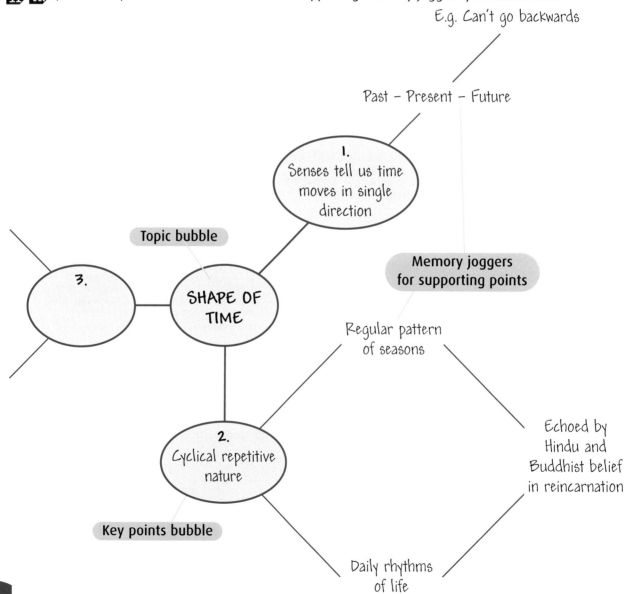

The Art of Information Writing

Learning from example

AIMS

- Identify the key ingredients of information text.

- Revisit the stylistic conventions of information text, focusing on techniques for making information accessible through using detail or example as appropriate.

- Think about how the writer has described customs in a way that is both accurate and interesting.

- Think about what sort of language choices make writing more effective.

In this section you will think about the key features of information text, the techniques writers use to make it accessible and the powerful words they choose to help inform the reader.

Test watch As well as building up your writing skills, the following sections are good preparation for the optional reading tests at the end of Year 7 because they help you to:

- comment on a writer's purpose and the effects of the text on the reader
- comment on the structure and organisation of texts
- comment on a writer's use of language
- deduce, infer or interpret information, events or ideas
- describe, select or retrieve information, events or ideas from texts.

If you show these skills in the reading test, you will gain a better mark.

Task 4 ## Reading

Below and on page 40 is the introduction and two entries from *Aliens in Flares! – An Amazing A–Z of Things They Never Tell You About Time,* a book aimed at young people visiting the Royal Observatory in Greenwich, London. The Royal Observatory is built around the Prime Meridian of Longitude, which has set our world time system since 1884.

While reading the extract, consider the following questions:

- Which features make this an information text?

- How have the writers tried to engage their audience? For example, how does the introduction hook the reader? Can you find examples from everyday life that relate to the reader's experience? How formal is the style?

The Art of Information Writing

What is Time?

Present tense

Introduction
– sums up key feature of time

Time **is** something which affects us all in many different ways. It also generates some of the most **intriguing questions asked by visitors** to the Royal Observatory Greenwich, the 'Home of time'.

Paragraphs – in logical order

This little A–Z book goes a long way to answering some of these questions and also **presents a whole range of other amazing facts and figures** which show the influence of time on our daily lives.

Formal language

Generalisation
– summing up a key point

Here are the first two entries under the letter D:

Dandelion clocks

Topic sentence – introduces key points

The **downy** head of the dandelion, which contains the seeds of the plant, is **traditionally** used by children as a game for guessing the time. By counting the number of **puffs** it takes to blow all the seeds off the stalk, children learn to **recite** the hours of the day. The game also helps to maintain the life **cycle** of the dandelion, by **scattering** the seeds and improving the plant's chances of **sprouting** the following year.

Technical vocabulary
– related to topic

Dates for the world

The Gregorian calendar is used throughout the world even though it is essentially a Christian version of an ancient Roman calendar. Many non-Christians use the Gregorian calendar but they also have their own calendars which reflect a yearly cycle of their own religious beliefs and festivals. **Whereas** the Gregorian system uses the phrase Anno Domini (AD) to date its years, Jewish people use the phrase 'Anno Mundi', meaning 'the year of the world'. This system is based on a belief that the world was created on what Christians would call 7 October 3761BC. **Muslims use** 'Anno Hijirae' counting their years from the Prophet Muhammad's emigration (Hijra) from Mecca to Medina on 16 July AD622. **In an attempt** to replace the Christian terms BC and AD, some people use abbreviations BCE (meaning before the common era) and CE (the common era).

(See also : Anno Domini: Gregorian Calendar; Year of Confusion)

Features of information text

The first half of the extract has been annotated to bring out some key features of information texts (see the panel on page 36). Topic sentences have also been highlighted in orange in paragraphs 1 to 3.

Annotating

Annotate the second half of the text to illustrate more examples of as many of these features as possible.

Making information accessible

The writers of *Aliens in Flares!* wanted to attract a young audience. Below is a list of techniques that writers often use to try and make information accessible to people.

Technique	Tick if used	Evidence
1. Introduction that hooks the readers' interest		
2. Simple language		
3. Technical terms explained in simple language		
4. Formal but friendly style		
5. Everyday examples to relate to the readers' knowledge/interests		
6. Detail to illustrate a point		
7. Engage reader through questions/intrigue		

Task 6 **Finding evidence**

Decide how many of the techniques in the grid have been used in the extract. Be prepared to support your conclusions with evidence.

How effective is the two-paragraph preface as an introduction to this book? Have evidence to support your view.

Choosing powerful words

The writers have selected powerful and descriptive words to inform us about dandelion clocks. Some of these words have been underlined in the extract so that you can consider them in context.

> **downy   traditionally   puffs   recite   cycle   scattering   sprouting**

Task 7 **Vocabulary**

Think of at least one other word that could be used in each case. Decide if your word or the original one is the more effective. Be prepared to present your findings with reasons to back up your choice.

3 Text structure and organisation

Getting the structure right

AIMS

- Use an information skeleton to note down the structure of the passage and its key content.

- Analyse how the writers have organised the information appropriately and signposted it clearly for the reader.

- Experiment with altering the structure of the writing to meet a different purpose.

In this section you will consider the structure of a passage and attempt to rewrite it from a different perspective.

Signposting information

Structuring writing clearly and 'signposting' how one section relates to another helps the reader to understand the text. Clear signposting is also needed within paragraphs to help the reader follow how ideas are grouped, connected or developed. Using these techniques makes a text cohesive (see the explanation on page 56).

Task 8 **Recording**

 Why do you think the information in the introduction to *Aliens in Flares!* has been divided into two paragraphs?

Can you think of an explanation why the entries themselves are not divided into paragraphs? Look at how the book is laid out on page 39 to help you.

Now read the *Dates for the World* entry below. The topic sentences indicating the focus of each section of this entry have been highlighted in orange for you.

The Gregorian calendar is used throughout the world even though it is essentially a Christian version of an ancient Roman calendar. Many non-Christians use the Gregorian calendar but they also have their own calendars which reflect a yearly cycle of their own religious beliefs and festivals. **Whereas** the Gregorian system uses the phrase Anno Domini (AD) to date its years, Jewish people use the phrase 'Anno Mundi', meaning 'the year of the world'. This system is based on a belief that the world was created on what Christians would call 7 October 3761BC. **Muslims use** 'Anno Hijirae' counting their years from the Prophet Muhammad's emigration (Hijra) from Mecca to Medina on 16 July AD622. **In an attempt** to replace the Christian terms BC and AD, some people use abbreviations BCE (meaning before the common era) and CE (the common era).

Structuring

Sketch an information skeleton, like the one below. Since there are four sections, you will need four bubbles, in addition to the topic bubble.

Complete the bubbles using a topic heading to sum up each section based on the topic sentences.

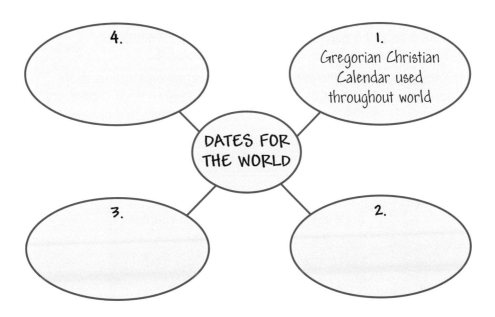

If you decided to paragraph this entry, how many paragraphs would you use?

As you can see, an information skeleton suggests where the paragraph or section breaks will come in a text. However, it does not help you decide what *order* to put those sections/paragraphs in (use the numbers to tell you the order).

Why do you think the writers began this entry with information about the Christian calendar?

Task 10 **Structuring**

The opening words of each of the four sections in the *Dates of the World* entry are:
- The Gregorian Calendar is used
- Whereas
- Muslims use
- In an attempt

How effective are these as signposts for the reader? Try out these alternative signposts. Decide if they work as well or better than the originals.
- The whole world uses
- While *or* Although
- However, Muslims use *or* On the other hand, Muslims use
- As a way of replacing *or* In order

The Art of Information Writing

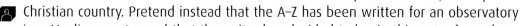
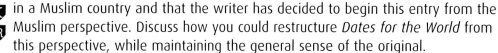

Dates for the World has been written for an observatory in a Western, mainly Christian country. Pretend instead that the A–Z has been written for an observatory in a Muslim country and that the writer has decided to begin this entry from the Muslim perspective. Discuss how you could restructure *Dates for the World* from this perspective, while maintaining the general sense of the original.

1 Jot down the order you would put the sections in.

2 Think about how you are going to begin the entry. For example:
The Muslim calendar is based on 'Anno Hijirae' because...

3 Decide how you are going to link this opening section on Muslims to the following sections. Jot down the phrase that will signpost each section if you have changed them in any way. (You could use the alternative phrases from Task 10 to help you.)

For example:

> The Muslim calendar is based on 'Anno Hijirae' because Muslims count their years from the Prophet Muhammad's emigration (Hijra) from Mecca to Medina on 16 July ad622.
>
> However, the Gregorian calendar is used throughout the world even though it is essentially a Christian version of an ancient Roman calendar. Many non-Christians use the Gregorian calendar but they also have their own calendars which reflect a yearly cycle of their own religious beliefs and festivals ...

4 Finally, read your entry through carefully to make certain the text hangs together logically and change any linking phrases as necessary.

Consider these questions and be prepared to feed back your response:

• What were the key difficulties in restructuring the text in this way?

• What makes it easier to start with the Gregorian calendar?

Sentence structure and punctuation

Making the sentences work

AIMS

- Use punctuation effectively to guide the reader through the meaning of sentences.

- Recognise the importance of using pronouns carefully so as not to confuse the reader.

In this section you will use pronouns and punctuation carefully, so that you help readers understand rather than confuse them.

Using punctuation to help the reader understand a text

Punctuation is essential to enable readers to understand a text easily. Full stops divide groups of words into chunks of meaning, while commas help the flow of a sentence by adding pauses.

Task 12 · Defining

 Match each punctuation mark to its function below. (Note: Some punctuation marks have more than one function.)

1 full stop .	**A** Marks the end of a sentence
2 colon :	**B** Separates words, phrases or clauses that provide extra information in a sentence; indicates pauses
3 semicolon ;	**C** Indicates that the sentence is a question
4 brackets ( )	**D** Used at the end of a line to show that a word continues on the next; links two words together to make a compound word; links a phrase together so that it can be used like an adjective
5 comma ,	**E** Indicates a pause in a sentence that is more significant than that indicated by a comma
6 hyphen -	**F** Indicates possession or a missing letter or letters
7 dash –	**G** Indicates that the sentence is an exclamation or command
8 elipsis …	**H** Marks a stronger pause than a semicolon and often links two closely related sentences; is used to introduce lists, explanations and sometimes quotations
10 question mark ?	**I** Represents a short pause, or is used instead of brackets or commas to separate off information in a sentence
11 apostrophe '	**J** Shows the beginning and end of direct speech, titles or quotations
12 exclamation mark !	**K** Indicates that text has been left out or is incomplete
13 speech marks/ inverted commas " "	**L** Separates items in a list when commas would be confusing

Task 13 — Explaining

Look again at the extract from *Aliens in Flares!* on page 40. Annotate the punctuation in it for another class of 12-year-olds. Try to explain the use of as many of the punctuation marks as you can. For example:

'Home of time' — Inverted commas indicate a title

Task 14 — Analysing

> ### GRAMMAR
>
> **Using pronouns carefully**
>
> Pronouns are words used to replace a noun, noun phrase or clause in order to avoid repetition. 'I', 'you', 'we', 'its', 'herself', 'this', 'that', 'who', 'which' and 'that' are all examples of pronouns.

Look at this rewritten entry for 'Dandelion clocks' where many nouns have been replaced by 'it', 'its', 'they' or 'them'. Discuss what the key problem is now with this paragraph.

> It is used throughout the world even though it is essentially their version of theirs. Many of them use their calendar but they also have theirs which reflect one of their own religious beliefs and festivals.

- Note down any problems that could arise when using too many pronouns.
- If you were writing advice about using pronouns, what would the advice be?

Composing effective sentences

Task 15 — Rewriting

Reread the opening paragraph of *Aliens in Flares!*, this time focusing on the sentence structure.

The writers have clearly chosen to keep their sentence structure fairly simple. Although all the sentences are complex sentences, e.g. (Time is something which affects us all in many different ways.), they feel fairly simple because each one begins with a main clause (underlined above) which helps orientate the reader. Now see what effect beginning this sentence with a subordinate clause has on the style of the passage.

- Rewrite the first paragraph using only one sentence. Try to maintain the original sense. Your paragraph should begin with 'Because'.
- Read your sentence through making certain that it flows coherently, that the pronouns are not confusing and that the punctuation helps make it clear.

5 Composing your own information text

AIMS

- Plan, draft and revise a coherent information text that has been composed to suit a particular audience, using a text skeleton to help you.

- Organise your ideas into coherent paragraphs using the first sentence to signpost the reader and developing and concluding them appropriately.

- Vary your sentence structure to add pace, variety and emphasis.

Your task

Write two brief entries for an A–Z of your school – the first is entitled 'The School Day'; the second is entitled 'The School Year'. Use what you have learned about information texts in this unit to help you.

Test watch This writing task is good preparation for the type of writing required in your English tests because it helps you learn how to:

- plan your work so that it is organised logically into well-constructed paragraphs that are linked together well

- compose your writing effectively to match its audience and purpose,

- and select powerful vocabulary

- vary the structure of your sentences and punctuate them correctly.

If you show these skills in the optional English test at the end of Year 7, you will gain a better mark.

1 Planning your structure

 Since you know who your audience is (new students and their parents) and the purpose of your writing task (a guide to the school), the important thing is to plan your writing. Think about what information to include and how to structure and link your ideas clearly.

For your two entries for the school's A–Z, you need to be clear about the content you want to include. The information you should include is listed in a random order.

- ★ When the day begins
- ★ When the day ends
- ★ The number of terms in a year
- ★ The number of lessons in a day
- ★ The length of lessons
- ★ The typical length of a half term (or term)
- ★ The length and time of the lunch hour
- ★ The length and time of any other breaks
- ★ The length of the holidays
- ★ Five staff training days

Use an information skeleton to help sketch out a plan before you start composing. Divide the information on page 47 into the two categories, using memory joggers to organise the relevant information appropriately within these categories. Link related information as indicated below.

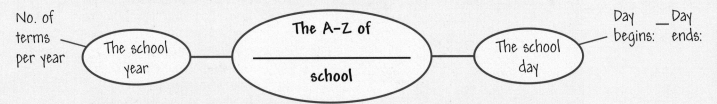

No. of terms per year — The school year — The A-Z of _____ school — The school day — Day begins: _ Day ends:

Decide whether you want to start with the school day or the school year. Remember, you may find you want to change this when composing the paragraphs. Imagine you've decided to begin with a paragraph on the school year. Look at all the information you've grouped together on the school year and decide which information it will be best to start with. You could begin with a topic sentence like this: The school year at Northfields is divided into terms – autumn, spring and summer. You may want to break the information on the school year into two paragraphs. If you do, make certain there is a logical reason for the break.

2 Discussing what you are going to write

Just before you start writing, talk through what you are going to write.

Check to see that your points flow clearly. Now you are ready to start writing.

Points to remember

As you write, remember to:

- order your points and paragraphs logically (see page 42).
- begin each paragraph with a topic sentence (see page 43).
- signpost the paragraphs clearly so the reader doesn't get lost (see page 44).
- select a formal but friendly style (see page 41).
- choose the right words (see page 41).
- vary your sentence structure while making your points clearly and simply (see page 46).
- check that your punctuation helps the reader follow the sense of your sentences (see page 45).
- check that the way you have used pronouns couldn't lead to confusion (see page 46).

Top tip When writing, it is often a good idea to picture the typical reader as you write, asking yourself if this reader will be able to understand what you are trying to say.

You may want to use some of the sentence signposts and connectives below to help you.

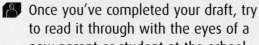

Sentence signposts and connectives

- A typical school term is
- In addition
- The school day begins
- Normally
- After the first two lessons

- Break lasts for
- The school year at X is divided into
- The day ends
- Straight after lunch

 Once you've completed your draft, try to read it through with the eyes of a new parent or student at the school. Ask yourself if an outsider would be able to understand it. Check that you have varied your sentences. Amend your text if necessary.

3 Peer comment

- Swap your draft with your partner's and read each other's carefully. Discuss what works well and highlight this on the drafts. Then discuss how you could improve particular sections. Jot down your suggestions on the draft.
- Redraft the parts of your A–Z where necessary, using your partner's comments to guide you.

4 Pulling it all together

- Listen to extracts from 'The school day' and 'The school year' written by members of your class.
- Decide what are the key features that make these information texts effective. Be prepared to feed your ideas back to the class.
- Set up to three targets for yourself for improving your next piece of information text.

D The Art of Explanation Writing

 **How explanation text works**

AIMS

- Revisit the key ingredients of explanation text.
- Analyse the structure of explanation text.

In this section you will build on your existing knowledge of how an explanation text works, thinking about its audience, purpose and form.

Audience, purpose, form

Explanation texts help you understand how or why things happen – showing how one thing can cause something else or how something works. Some typical examples of explanation texts are:

- **car manuals**, such as *Haynes Car Guides*
- **encyclopedias**, such as the *Encyclopaedia Britannica*
- **science textbooks**, such as *Science Directions.*

Try not to confuse explanation texts with information texts. An information text tells you about the key characteristics of things (what they are like) rather than what causes them.

TYPICAL FEATURES

The typical features of explanation texts are listed below. You will need to refer to these in Section 2.

- The **audience** is someone who wants to understand a process.
- Its **purpose** is to help someone understand a process.
- The **form** or structure that an explanation text often takes is as a series of logical steps (often paragraphs) explaining how or why something occurs (this is known as cause and effect), with topic sentences introducing each step.

Typical **language features** of explanation texts are:

- causal[1] language including causal connectives, e.g. 'because'
- technical, precise vocabulary, e.g. 'tilt of the Earth on its axis'
- formal and impersonal language, e.g. 'The North Pole always points'
- present tense, e.g. 'is tilted'

[1] **causal** – stating or implying a cause

Reading and annotating

 The start of the extract *The Seasons* has been annotated to illustrate all the language
[X] [TR] features of an explanation text. Read the extract and the annotations carefully, then
annotate the second half to show where the same elements occur.

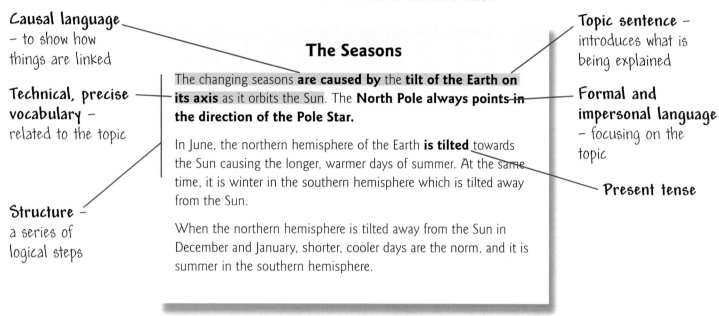

Causal language – to show how things are linked

Technical, precise vocabulary – related to the topic

Structure – a series of logical steps

Topic sentence – introduces what is being explained

Formal and impersonal language – focusing on the topic

Present tense

The Seasons

The changing seasons **are caused by** the **tilt of the Earth on its axis** as it orbits the Sun. The **North Pole always points in the direction of the Pole Star.**

In June, the northern hemisphere of the Earth **is tilted** towards the Sun causing the longer, warmer days of summer. At the same time, it is winter in the southern hemisphere which is tilted away from the Sun.

When the northern hemisphere is tilted away from the Sun in December and January, shorter, cooler days are the norm, and it is summer in the southern hemisphere.

Topic sentences

Topic sentences are used to introduce the key focus of each paragraph. They are often the first sentence of a paragraph. If you summarise the topic sentences, you get a picture of the whole passage.

Task 2 Summarising

 Complete the summary below by adding the focus of the last paragraph.

[X] Paragraph 1: Seasons caused by Earth tilting as it orbits Sun
Paragraph 2: When northern hemisphere is tilted towards Sun, it's warmer
Paragraph 3:

Using text skeletons

In order to understand the structure of a text, it can be useful to draw a diagram or 'text skeleton'. Text skeletons represent the bare bones of a text.

A typical explanation skeleton, showing how one thing leads to another, is given on page 52. Each bubble represents one stage in the explanation. In this case there are three stages organised into three paragraphs, so there are three bubbles on the skeleton. The notes in each bubble give the focus of the paragraph, for example 'Seasons caused by Earth tilting as it orbits Sun'. The lines branching from each bubble are its key related points, for example 'North Pole always points towards Pole Star'. These notes are known as memory joggers.

Using text skeletons will help you to analyse the structure of a text and plan your own writing.

The Art of Explanation Writing

Structuring

Below is a partially-completed text skeleton for *The Seasons*. Work together to
X TR complete the key point and memory joggers that sum up the final paragraph.

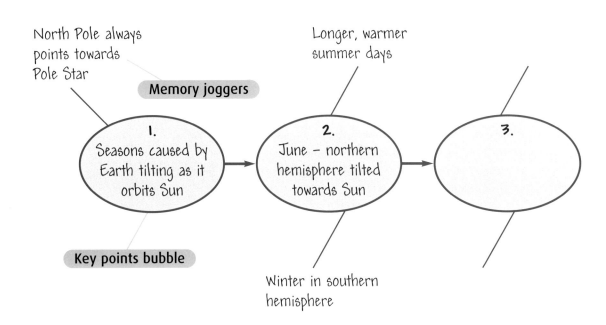

North Pole always
points towards
Pole Star

Longer, warmer
summer days

Memory joggers

1.
Seasons caused by
Earth tilting as it
orbits Sun

2.
June – northern
hemisphere tilted
towards Sun

3.

Key points bubble

Winter in southern
hemisphere

Learning from example

AIMS

- Consider how writers keep tense usage consistent, managing changes of tense so that meaning is clear.

- Consider how writers vary the structure of sentences to suit purpose.

- Deploy words with precision, including their exact implication in context.

- Think about how writers can help make complex ideas understandable.

In this section you will focus on an explanation text and think about what techniques the writer has used to help the reader understand the process described, as well as engaging the reader's interest.

Test watch   As well as building up your writing skills, the following sections are good preparation for the optional reading tests at the end of Year 7 because they help you to:

- comment on a writer's purpose and the effects of the text on the reader

- comment on the structure and organisation of texts

- comment on a writer's use of language

- deduce, infer or interpret information, events or ideas

- describe, select or retrieve information, events or ideas from texts.

If you show these skills in the reading test, you will gain a better mark.

Making things clear

This is the final entry in *Aliens in Flares! – An Amazing A–Z of Things They Never Tell You About Time*, a title aimed at young people visiting the Royal Observatory in Greenwich, London.

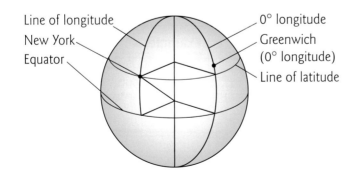

New York is 73° 50' west of Greenwich. This means that noon in New York occurs nearly five hours after it occurs in Greenwich.

Task 4   **Annotating**

The first half of the explanation text on page 54 has been annotated to illustrate all the features of explanation texts, given on page 50. Read the text and annotations carefully. Annotate the second half to bring out all these features.

The Art of Explanation Writing

Zero Longitude

Present tense

Technical, precise vocabulary – related to the topic

Formal and impersonal language – in this case including the passive – focusing on the topic

Structure – Series of logical steps

Topic sentence – introduces what is being explained

Causal language – to show how things are linked

Longitude **is** essential to the measurement of time around the world. **The lines of longitude and latitude are** <u>familiar</u> **from atlases and maps**. They create an imaginary <u>grid</u> which can be used to <u>pinpoint</u> any location on the surface of the Earth.

What many people do not realise is that the measurement of longitude (position east or west) is <u>directly</u> related to the measurement of time. The Earth takes 24 hours to complete one full <u>revolution</u> of 360°. **This means that** in one hour, the Earth revolves one twenty-fourth of a spin, or 15°, or that in 4 minutes it revolves 1°, and so on. This was an important fact for early explorers who found it impossible to <u>navigate</u> a ship while out of sight of land.

To calculate longitude at sea, a navigator needs to know two things: what time is it <u>on board</u> ship, which can be measured using the Sun, and what time it is back home. The time difference converts into a longitude difference.

Knowing the time back home was the biggest problem because there was no clock available which could cope with keeping <u>accurate</u> time on a rolling ship. Many ideas were put forward for <u>solving</u> the 'longitude problem' which was the greatest scientific puzzle of the age.

Using language effectively

Good writers can explain complex processes in clear language. Below is a list of features that writers often use to help readers grasp complex ideas more easily.

Task 5 · Recording

Find at least one example of each feature in the extract. Use your annotations to help you. Jot down your quotations on a grid like the one below.

Feature that makes text easier to understand	Example
1. Using simple sentences to sum key points up clearly	Longitude is essential to the measurement of time around the world
2. Using a formal but friendly style	
3. Referring to things the reader may already know	
4. Using powerful words that precisely describe the process or idea being focused on (already underlined)	
5. Explaining technical vocabulary	
6. Including examples to help the reader understand potentially complex points	

Controlling tense to suit purpose

The writer's art is to understand the purpose of the text and to compose their writing to suit it. The explanation text *Zero Longitude* does not use the present tense throughout; some sentences are in the past tense.

Task 6 **Analysing** ━━━━━━━━━━

 Reread the passage on page 54. Identify the paragraph that is in the past tense, plus the one other sentence in the past tense.

Explain why the past tense has been used in these two instances. What does the past tense add to your understanding of why longitude is essential to the measurement of time around the world?

Selecting powerful words

Effective writing often relies on selecting the most appropriate word or phrase to describe exactly what is being explained. Ten such powerful and precise words or phrases have been underlined in the text and listed below.

> **familiar   grid   pinpoint   directly   revolution   navigate**
> **on board   converts   accurate   solving**

Task 7 **Finding alternative words** ━━━━━━━━━━

 Use a dictionary to help you explain the meaning of each word in its context.

Now use a dictionary or thesaurus to see if you can come up with an equally appropriate or even more effective word to replace each of those underlined, without changing the meaning of the text. Be prepared to present any alternative words you have found or defend the words selected by the writer.

Text structure and organisation

Getting the structure right

AIMS

- Consider how the writer has organised explanation text logically and signposted this clearly using causal connectives.

- Analyse how the writer has developed ideas and explained a process logically, highlighting the links between cause and effect.

- Recognise cues to start a new paragraph and how the first sentence orientates readers.

- Note down the key points of a text.

In this section you will consider the structure of an explanation text and consider what devices the writer has used to ensure the explanation is coherent and cohesive.

Signposting explanation

Structuring writing clearly and 'signposting' how one section relates to another helps the reader to understand the text. Clear signposting is also needed within paragraphs to help the reader follow how ideas are grouped, connected or developed. These features make a text cohesive.

One of the key techniques for making a text cohesive is to use the opening sentence of each paragraph to help orientate the reader: either to show how the new paragraph relates to the previous paragraph or to introduce the focus of the new paragraph. Such sentences are often known as topic sentences. Using these techniques makes a text cohesive.

Task 8 **Analysing**

Below are the opening sentences or clauses for each of the four paragraphs of *Zero Longitude*. Discuss the role of each of these sentences within the text.

Opening sentences or clauses of paragraphs	Role within text
Longitude is essential to the measurement of time around the world.	
What many people do not realise is that the measurement of longitude (position east or west) is directly related to the measurement of time.	
To calculate longitude at sea, a navigator needs to know two things:	
Knowing the time back home was the biggest problem.	

TYPICAL FEATURES

Coherence is the overall consistency of a text and how it hangs together as a whole. Organising your ideas by using paragraphs, subheadings, layout conventions and presentational devices makes a text coherent.

Cohesion is how individual sections of text hang together and relate to the sections around them. References back, contrasts, connectives and sentence signposts are some of the signals that make a text cohesive.

The Art of Explanation Writing

Planning the structure

Task 9 ## Structuring

Sketch out a text skeleton to represent the *Zero Longitude* explanation. Use topic sentences to help you sum up the focus of the missing sections 2 and 4.

Decide how to lay out the memory joggers for sections 2 and 4 to best sum up the text.

Time difference = longitude difference

Imaginary grid – pinpoints anywhere on Earth

i. Time on ship   ii. Time back home

1. Longitude essential to measurement of time around world

2.

3. To calculate longitude at sea, navigator needs to know two things

4.

Practising explanation writing

A pupil has got this simple maths addition wrong because she has jumbled up the tens and units. The answer should be 296.

$$\begin{array}{r} 159 \\ 40 \\ 97 \\ \hline 260 \end{array} \; \textbf{X}$$

Task 10 ## Planning practice

Explain in two paragraphs, as clearly and precisely as possible, what caused the problem and what the pupil should have done instead.

Below are some useful sentence signposts and connectives. Decide which two will start the topic sentences that will open your two paragraphs. Then list all five in a logical order for the explanation.

Sentence signposts and connectives
- Then she would have
- She should have
- The pupil got the wrong answer because she has
- Instead of putting
- As a result, when she

Before you begin to draft your paragraphs, practise talking through your explanation.

Make certain you use tenses appropriately.

The Art of Explanation Writing

Sentence structure and punctuation

Making the sentences work

AIMS

- Examine why the passive voice often suits explanation text.

- Extend your use, control and punctuation of complex sentences.

In this section you will focus on what difference the passive voice makes to sentences, and on constructing sentences effectively to suit the needs of an explanation text.

GRAMMAR

Using the passive to focus on the action not the actor

In active sentences the subject performs the action described by the verb.

Subject   Verb (action)

Many people put forward **ideas** about how to solve the longitude problem.

Object

In passive sentences the subject is on the receiving end of the action.

Subject

Many ideas were put forward about how to solve the longitude problem.

Verb (action)

One effect of using the passive is to make the text more impersonal. Look at these examples of passive sentences from the extract.

1. The lines of longitude and latitude are familiar from atlases and maps.

Active version: You are probably familiar with the lines of longitude and latitude from atlases and maps.

2. The time difference converts into a longitude difference.

Active version: You can convert the time difference into a longitude difference.

Task 11 **Practising the passive**

Rewrite the following passage so that it is in the passive.

I heated **the mixture** until it was boiling. I recorded **the length of time it took to reach boiling point** and repeated **the process** three times. Finally, I wrote up **the experiment**.

Top tip   Bring the object of the verb to the front of the sentence and make it the subject of the sentence. Leave out the person who is doing all these things. To help you, the object of the sentences has been written in bold. You may want to begin like this:

The mixture was heated until...

Writing and punctuating complex sentences

Task 12 **Analysing sentences**

Look at the sentence structure of paragraph 2 below. The sentences have been colour-coded to match the type of sentences that have been used. (For a key to the colour coding, see page 146.)

> What many people do not realise is that the measurement of longitude (position east or west) is directly related to the measurement of time. The Earth takes 24 hours to complete one full revolution of 360°. This means that, in one hour, the Earth revolves one twenty-fourth of a spin, or 15°, or that in 4 minutes it revolves 1°, and so on. This was an important fact for early explorers who found it impossible to **navigate** a ship while out of sight of land.

Below, the same paragraph has been mostly rewritten in simple sentences (one clause per sentence).

> The measurement of longitude is directly related to the measurement of time. This refers to its position east or west. Many people do not realise this. The Earth takes 24 hours to complete one full revolution of 360°. In one hour, the Earth revolves one twenty-fourth of a spin. This could be expressed as 15°. In 4 minutes it revolves 1°. This was an important fact for early explorers. They found it impossible to **navigate** a ship while out of sight of land.

What is the effect of using too many simple sentences on the meaning of the paragraph? Explain why complex sentences are so important when cause and effect are being explained. You may want to begin your answers like this:

- The simple sentences mean that there aren't any ...
- Clauses like 'this means that' help the reader to ...

Be prepared to discuss your ideas.

Task 13 **Analysing punctuation**

Now look at the way paragraph 3 has been punctuated.

> To calculate longitude at sea, a navigator needs to know two things: what time is it on board ship, which can be measured using the Sun, and what time it is back home. The time difference converts into a longitude difference.

Explain the function of each piece of punctuation in this paragraph. Be prepared to present your explanations.

The Art of Explanation Writing

AIMS

- Plan, draft and revise the story with reader and purpose in mind.

- Develop ideas and explain a process logically, highlighting the links between cause and effect.

- Organise ideas into a coherent sequence of paragraphs, introducing, developing and concluding the ideas appropriately.

- Write an explanation using the present tense and impersonal voice where appropriate, and linking the points clearly.

Your task

Write a clear explanation of British Standard Time, bringing out the links between cause and effect. Use what you have learned about explanation texts in this unit to help you.

Test watch This writing task is good preparation for the type of writing required in your English tests because it helps you learn how to:

- plan your work so that it is organised logically into well-constructed paragraphs which are linked together well

- compose your writing effectively to match its audience and purpose,

- and select powerful vocabulary

- vary the structure of your sentences and punctuate them correctly.

If you show these skills in the optional English test at the end of Year 7, you will gain a better mark.

1 Audience, purpose and form

Your task is to write a brief explanation of British Standard Time, including why clocks are moved forward one hour in the spring and back in the autumn. Your audience is a class of ten-year-olds who may find the whole concept rather complicated. Try to think of real-life examples which they can relate to which will help them to understand the explanation and engage their interest.

2 Considering the content

 Read the key information on page 61 about British Summer Time. It has been divided into four sections. The information in each block is in no particular order and is mainly written in simple sentences. This means there is no logical order and no signposts to help the reader.

Why Do We Change The Clocks Twice a Year?

Introduction:
The clocks are changed twice a year. Many people don't know why.
They also can't remember whether the clocks move backwards or forwards in spring and autumn.

British Summer Time	Greenwich Mean Time
The clock goes forward an hour for the summer.	In the winter it goes back an hour.
The evenings are lighter.	Wintertime is known as Greenwich
The mornings are darker.	Mean Time (GMT).
The sun rises an hour later. Most people are still asleep then.	There is much less daylight in the
British Standard Time (BST) was originally introduced as a wartime	wintertime.
measure in 1916. It promoted the efficient use of daylight.	GMT makes it lighter in the mornings
BST maximises the amount of useful daylight.	but the evenings are darker.

Reminder: A useful saying to help you remember which way the clocks move is: spring
FORWARD; fall (autumn) BACK.

3 Planning the structure

Since you already know your audience (ten-year-old pupils) and the purpose of the writing task (to explain why clocks are moved forward and backward), the first thing you need to do is to plan your writing. Consider how to structure it and how to link your ideas clearly. This will help the reader follow the explanation and help you express it.

- Use an explanation skeleton to help sketch out a plan. This sample skeleton includes an overall introduction followed by two linked pieces of explanation, one for BST and one for GMT, and a conclusion.
- Complete the skeleton to help you sort out where to fit in each piece of information.

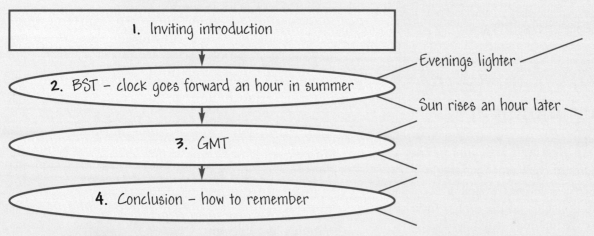

1. Inviting introduction

2. BST – clock goes forward an hour in summer — Evenings lighter — Sun rises an hour later

3. GMT

4. Conclusion – how to remember

- Once you have organised your ideas, decide how you are going to compose the account both to interest your reader and provide a clear explanation.

4 Discussing what you are going to write

Practise talking through what you think you are going to write for each stage before you start writing. Help each other to express the explanation clearly.

Now you are ready to start writing.

Points to remember

As you write, remember to:

- think about your audience (ten-year-olds).
- use topic sentences to guide the reader (see page 56).
- use language and references that help the reader understand (see page 54).
- select precise words and explain any technical terms (see page 55).
- keep the sentences as straightforward as possible while bringing out the causal links (see page 59).

- use the present tense as the main tense but use other tenses, where appropriate (see page 55).
- keep the style formal but friendly (see page 54).
- use causal connectives to bring out the consequences of the change in the clocks (see page 59).
- use the passive if it helps makes the explanation clear (see page 58).

You may want to use some of the sentence signposts and connectives below to help you.

Sentence signposts and connectives

- Many of us get confused about whether the clocks move backward or
- Many of us get confused about why
- The reason why we have British Standard Time
- By changing the clock so that
- Of course this also means that
- because
- BST was originally introduced
- British Standard Time (BST) maximises the amount
- Wintertime is known as Greenwich Mean Time (GMT) when

- In winter time
- This causes
- If you want an easy way
- This means that

 ## 5 Peer comment

Swap your draft with your partner's and read each other's carefully. Discuss what works well and highlight this on the drafts. Then discuss how you could improve

particular sections. Jot down your suggestions on the draft.

Redraft the parts of your explanation where necessary, using your partner's comments to guide you.

6 Pulling it all together

Listen to some of the explanations written by members of your class.

Decide what are the key features that make these information texts

effective. Be prepared to feed your ideas back to the class.

Set up to three targets for yourself for improving the next explanation text you write.

E The Art of Instruction Writing

How instruction text works

AIMS

- Revisit the key ingredients of instruction text.
- Analyse the structure of instruction text.

You are going to build on your knowledge of how an instruction text works, thinking about its audience, purpose and form, as well as focusing on its structure and language features.

Audience, purpose, form

Instruction texts tell you how to do something. Some examples are:

- **recipe books**, for example, *The Complete Book of Curries*
- **instruction manuals**, for example, *The Book of Bike Maintenance.*

TYPICAL FEATURES

The typical features of instruction texts are listed below. You will need to refer to these in Section 2.

- The **audience** is someone who wants to know how to do something.
- Its **purpose** is to tell someone how to do something clearly.
- The **form** or structure of instructions often includes chronological order, visual aids or layout to help the reader follow instructions, a list format to make sequence clear, and diagrams instead of description.

Typical **language features** of instruction texts are:

- simple, clear, brief formal English, e.g. 'DAY – DATE – MONTH – HOUR – MINUTE'
- technical language where necessary, e.g. 'validated permit'
- imperative tense beginning each order – this also helps underline the sequence, e.g. 'validate permit'
- often includes a diagram to help visualise the instructions.

Task 1 · **Reading and annotating**

The start of an extract on parking permits has been annotated to illustrate all the language features of an information text on page 64.

Read the text and the annotations carefully, then annotate the second half to show where the same elements occur.

Why has the writer used capital letters for the last paragraph?

INSTRUCTIONS AND CONDITIONS

HOURS OF OPERATION:
MONDAY - SATURDAY
9.00 a.m. - 8.00p.m.
(Unless indicated otherwise
by signs on street).

Day
Date
Month
Hour
Minute

Upon arrival, validate permit
by scratching off five panels on
the parking permit(s). DAY - DATE
- MONTH - HOUR - MINUTE
(to next five minutes), to indicate
your arrival time.

Attach the clearly validated permit inside your vehicle window
nearest the kerb, calendar face outwards, so that it can easily
be read from outside your vehicle.

MAXIMUM PERMITTED STAY IS 4 HOURS
More than one permit may be displayed in order to show your
selected parking period. In this case the permits must be marked
identically and placed side by side.

MAKE SURE THE PARKING ATTENDANT CAN READ THE
FRONT OF YOUR PARKING PERMIT(S) FROM OUTSIDE
THE VEHICLE.
You are liable to a Penalty Charge Notice and your vehicle may
also be clamped or removed if you:

- indicate false arrival information.
- do not display a validated permit when parking
  in the Hampstead Residential Parking zone.
- display further permits after arrival.
- return to the same parking place within 1 hour.
- park beyond the time initially purchased.

Imperative tense – begins instructions, making orders clear

Diagram accompanies text (often replacing description) – to help the reader understand

Day
Date
Month
Hour
Minute

Chronological order – makes clear the order in which things should be done

---

Visitors' Parking Permit[1]

Upon arrival, <u>validate</u>[2] permit **by scratching off five panels on the parking permit, DAY – DATE – MONTH – HOUR – MINUTE** (to next five minutes), to indicate your arrival time.

<u>Attach the clearly</u> **validated permit** inside your vehicle window nearest the kerb, calendar face outwards.

MAKE SURE THE PARKING ATTENDANT CAN READ THE FRONT OF YOUR PARKING PERMIT FROM OUTSIDE THE VEHICLE

Simple, clear, brief, formal English – to help reader understand

Capital letters – to help reader notice key points

Technical language – where necessary

[1] **permit** – licence, official document giving permission
[2] **validate** – to confirm, to give official backing

Using text skeletons

In order to understand the structure of a text, it can be useful to draw a diagram or 'text skeleton'. Text skeletons represent the bare bones of a text.

A typical instruction skeleton looks like a timeline marked with clear stages. Each bubble represents a key point in the instructions. The notes inside these bubbles (e.g. 'Validate permit on arrival') are the key points or stages and the notes linked to the bubbles (e.g. 'Scratch off five panels: day - date - month - hour - minute') are known as memory joggers.

Task 2 **Structuring**

Below is a half-completed instruction text skeleton for *Visitors' Parking Permit*.
Discuss the key points and related memory joggers that you would add to bubble 3 to complete the skeleton.

Scratch off five panels:
day – date – month –
hour – minute

Calendar faces
outwards

Memory joggers

1.
Validate permit on arrival

2.
Attach permit inside vehicle window nearest kerb

3.

Key points bubble

2 Composition and effect

Learning from example

In this section you will look at four different attempts to write clear instructions and decide which one is best. You will also consider the nature of descriptive writing and how it contrasts with instructions.

Test watch As well as building up your writing skills, the following sections are good preparation for the optional reading tests at the end of Year 7 because they help you to:

- comment on a writer's purpose and the effects of the text on the reader
- comment on the structure and organisation of texts
- comment on a writer's use of language
- deduce, infer or interpret information, events or ideas
- describe, select or retrieve information, events or ideas from texts.

If you show these skills in the reading test, you will gain a better mark.

Audience and purpose

Writing effective instructions relies on thinking about the audience and purpose of the instructions, and choosing the right ingredients to make the instructions clear.

Task 3 **Analysing**

 Below and on page 66 are four different attempts to write clear instructions on how to set the alarm on an alarm clock. Decide which is best and how you would annotate it to show why it is a good example of instruction writing. The panel of features for instruction text on page 63 will help you.

Version 1

To set the alarm, I slid the set switch (1) to the ALARM SET position. Then I pressed the HOUR button (2) several times until the correct time (07) was displayed. After that, I pressed the MINUTE button (4) several times until it reached 00. Finally, I slid the SET switch (1) back to the run position.

Version 2

To set the alarm:

1. Slide the set switch 1 to the ALARM SET position.
2. Press the HOUR button 2 as many times as necessary for the correct time to be displayed.
3. PRESS the MINUTE button 4 as many times as necessary for the correct time to be displayed.
4. Slide the SET switch 1 back to the run position.

Version 3

How not to set the alarm

In the pursuit of punctuality, a new alarm clock beamed by my bed. Perhaps I muddled up the instructions for setting the time with those for setting the alarm. I had spent some time peering wearily at the diagram and cheerfully pressed a few things in the misplaced hope that the alarm would sound at seven.

Romantic dreams exploded into the panic of reality when the alarm chose instead to wake at 8:30. I flailed at it in horror like a drowning man. Detention loomed; even worse the relentless reprimands of a cynical tutor were already running through my mind.

Version 4

To set the alarm:

1. The first thing you have to do is to slide the set switch (see fig. 1 on the diagram) to the ALARM SET position.
2. The next thing you do is to press the HOUR button (see fig. 2 on the diagram) as many times as necessary for the correct time to be displayed.
3. After that, press the MINUTE button (see fig. 4 on the diagram) as many times as necessary for the correct time to be displayed.
4. The final thing to do is to slide the SET switch 1 back to the run position.

Task 4 · Analysing

Which version would be best if the writing task had been to write an amusing description of trying to set an alarm? Be prepared to present your conclusion.

Descriptive writing

Descriptive writing and figurative language are both common features of many types of text. It is often assumed that they are used in narrative and recount writing rather than texts like information or explanation. In fact, selecting just the right words to describe something powerfully is a central ingredient of most forms of writing.

X Below are some typical language features of descriptive writing. They include:

- powerful words (nouns, verbs, adverbs and adjectives) that help the reader understand exactly what is being described
- relevant detail to recreate the scene, but not so much as to become boring
- figurative language including imagery such as metaphors, similes and personification to help the reader picture the scene
- sound effects like repetition, alliteration and assonance to help create the atmosphere of what is being described
- varied sentence structure and punctuation to help maintain the reader's interest.

Top tip It is important not to overuse these features. For example, too much detail can make writing boring, and too much imagery can make writing too fussy.

TYPICAL FEATURES

Alliteration – the effect created when adjacent or closely connected words begin with the same letter or sound, e.g. 'silent slithering snakes'

Assonance – the effect created by the repetition of vowel sounds, e.g. 'green fields'

Metaphor – a form of imagery when one thing is said to be another, e.g. 'His piggy eyes...'

Personification – a form of imagery when an inanimate object is described in language that relates to humans or animals, e.g. 'The leaves whispered'

Repetition – repeating a word, phrase or sentence for a particular effect, e.g. 'Break, break, break,/On thy cold grey stones, O sea!'

Simile – a form of imagery when one thing is compared to another, e.g. 'He had eyes like a pig's'

- Reread version 3 of the alarm clock extracts and see if you can find one to two different sorts of effective examples of each of these ingredients. Be prepared to present your findings.

Task 6 **Writing**

 Imagine the strongest storm that you can. Brainstorm all the words that help recreate the image of this storm. Draft a short paragraph recreating the power of the wind and rain, etc., including figurative language and sound effects. Redraft your paragraph so that you have created exactly the image you wanted.

Task 7 **Reviewing**

 If you could offer only three pieces of advice to someone about to compose some instructions, what would they be? Why do you think figurative language is not a feature of instruction writing? What are the key differences between instructions and descriptive writing? Be prepared to present your findings.

The Art of Instruction Writing

Getting the structure right

AIMS

- Think about how to sequence and signpost instructions effectively.

- Consider how to give instructions that are easy to follow and clearly sequenced.

In this section you will see the devices used by the writer to ensure the instructions are organised as clearly as possible.

Signposting instructions

Structuring writing clearly and signposting how one section relates to another helps the reader to understand the text. Using there techniques makes a text coherent and cohesive (see the explanation on page 56).

Task 8 **Annotating**

 Look at version 2 of setting an alarm clock below. One feature used by the writer to structure this text coherently has been annotated for you.

Decide what other features the writer has used and note them down. You may want to look back at the list of features for instruction texts on page 63 to help you.

Layout – use of headings to make purpose clear

To set the alarm

1. Slide the set switch 1 to the ALARM SET position.
2. Press the HOUR button 2 as many times as necessary for the correct time to be displayed.
3. Press the MINUTE button 4 as many times as necessary for the correct time to be displayed.
4. Slide the SET switch 1 back to the run position.

Task 9 **Planning practice**

 Choose an activity listed below that you think you know how to do well.

 • Getting a cat into a cat basket (to take to the vet)

- Mending a puncture

- Making a cup of tea

- Blowing up a balloon

List each action in the order you think it should be done. For example:

1. Open the cat basket.
2. Put on protective clothing, especially gloves.

Making the sentences work

AIMS

- Identify, using appropriate terminology, the way writers of instructions match language and organisation to suit their purpose.

- Keep tense usage consistent, and manage changes of tense so that meaning is clear.

- Revise the language conventions of instruction text including imperative verbs and simple brief language.

In this section you will consider the most effective way to compose the sentences in instructions to make them clear.

Using the imperative

Using imperatives is a key feature of instruction texts because they tell the reader what to do.

GRAMMAR

The imperative is the form of a verb used to give orders, for example: '<u>Slide</u> the set switch 1 to the ALARM SET position', '<u>Stop</u> talking', '<u>Keep off</u> the grass!' The word 'imperative' comes from the same root as 'emperor' and 'imperial' – they are all concerned with giving orders. Normally the imperative is placed at the beginning of the sentence so that the instructions are clear.

Task 10 **Writing**

 Rewrite the statement below as instructions on how to make tea.

> The kettle <u>is filled</u> with water and <u>switched</u> on. A teabag <u>is placed</u> in each cup. When the water has boiled, it <u>is poured</u> into each cup until the cup is nearly full. Finally a small amount of milk <u>is added</u> to each cup.

All the verbs that need turning into the imperative have been underlined. Be prepared to present your instructions. Begin like this:

Fill the kettle with water and...

Top tip Talk through what you are going to write before you write it down, checking that it sounds like instructions.

The Art of Instruction Writing

Keeping your language simple and brief

Annotating

 The purpose of an instruction text is to explain how to do something as clearly and briefly as possible. Reread the alarm clock instructions, focusing on:

- how each stage has been signposted
- the use of complex sentences.

It may help to compare the new version below with version 2 on page 66. Be prepared to feed back your findings.

> To set the alarm, **first** slide the set switch (in the middle of the left-hand side of the clock) to the ALARM SET position. **The next thing** to do is press the HOUR button (marked with an H at the bottom of the clock on the left-hand side) several times until the correct time (07, for example) is displayed. **After that**, press the MINUTE button (marked with an M next to the H button) several times until it reaches 00. **The last thing** you have to do is slide the SET switch back to the run position.

Task 12 **Writing**

 Now rewrite the instructions below so they are as clear and brief as possible. You may want to begin like this:

1 **Find** the cat basket and...

Top tip Run through in your head what you are going to write before you write it.

> The first thing to do is to find the cat basket and open it so it is ready to hold the cat. In case the cat starts to scratch when it realises you are trying to put it in the basket, the next thing to do is to find some protective clothing, especially gloves. It's a good idea to take the basket into the room where the cat is and shut the door so it can't bolt and hide. Now pick up the cat, holding it away from you so you are out of reach of its claws, and put it inside the basket. Only let go of the cat when you have almost shut the lid.

Reread your draft and amend it. Remember, you are trying to write well-sequenced, clear, simple instructions using as few words as possible.

AIMS

- Write instructions that are precise, easy to follow, well signposted and clearly sequenced.

- Plan, draft, edit and revise instructions with reader and purpose in mind.

- Write an effective description that contrasts with the instuctions.

Your task

Write clear directions about how to get from your home to school, using what you have learned in this unit to help you. Then write a lively description about an aspect of your journey to school.

Test watch This writing task is good preparation for the type of writing required in your English tests because it helps you learn how to:

- plan your work so that it is organised logically into well-constructed paragraphs that are linked together well

- compose your writing effectively to match its audience and purpose,

- and select powerful vocabulary

- vary the structure of your sentences and punctuate them correctly.

If you show these skills in the optional English test at the end of Year 7, you will gain a better mark.

1 Audience and purpose

Your audience is someone who does not know the area. Discuss the effect the audience and purpose will have on the style of your directions. In particular, consider:

- Should the directions be vague or precise?

- Should the language be formal or informal?

- Should the language be simple or figurative?

- How can you reassure the reader that they are going in the right direction?

2 Working out the content

You obviously know your route to school very well, but remember that it will not be familiar to your audience. You must explain it so that a stranger could follow the route. Visualise all the stages, for example which way you turn when you leave your home. Remember to include landmarks that will reassure your reader that they are on the right track.

The Art of Instruction Writing

71

Planning the structure

 Text skeletons are very useful tools to help structure your writing. Use them to help you sketch out a plan before you start composing. Use an instruction skeleton to sum up the sequence of your route to school.

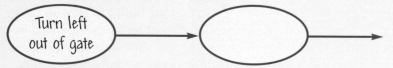

Turn left out of gate

 ## Composing your own instructions

 Decide how you are going to compose your instructions to maximise their clarity. Now you are ready to start wiriting.

Points to remember

As you write, remember to:

- think about your audience (see pages 65–66)
- sequence your directions chronologically (see page 68)
- lay out your information to bring out this order (see page 68)
- begin each instruction with a command – the imperative (see page 68)
- signpost your directions clearly (see page 68)
- choose precise simple words and sentence structure (see pages 69–70)
- keep your directions as brief as possible (see pages 69–70)
- use diagrams to help your reader where necessary (see page 65).

You may want to adapt some of the sentence signposts and connectives below to help you.

Sentence signposts and connectives

- Take the third turn on the
- Catch a number X bus
- After about a hundred metres
- When you reach X Street,
- Get off at
- The school is the large flat-roofed building
- The bus stop is on your
- The Kings Arms is on your
- Continue on this road until
- The visitors' entrance is
- Cross at the crossing and

 ## Discussing what you are going to write

Talk through what you think you are going to write for each stage.

Help each other to express each stage of the journey clearly.

6 Peer comment

- Once you've completed your draft, try to read it through the eyes of someone who has never made this journey. Will they be able to follow your instructions?
- Now swap your drafts. Discuss what really works well and highlight this on your draft.

- Decide what needs to be done to improve your directions and jot down up to three suggestions on the draft.
- Redraft the selected sections using these comments to guide you.

7 Pulling it all together

- Listen to extracts from the instructions written by members of your class.
- Decide what are the key features that make these information texts effective. Be prepared to feed your ideas back to the class.

- Set up to three targets for yourself for improving your next piece of instruction writing.

8 Taking your text in a different direction

Imagine that, instead of providing instructions for how to get from home to school, you have to *describe* your journey.

Use the list of features for description from page 67 and the following pointers as a guide to writing a short description of your route.

Points to remember

As you write, remember to:
- begin in a striking manner
- use powerful words that describe exactly the action or atmosphere
- include relevant detail but without using too much detail
- use figurative language and sound effects to bring the scene to life
- vary sentence structure.

F The Art of Persuasive Writing

How persuasion text works

AIMS

Revisit the key ingredients of persuasion text.

Use text skeletons to help analyse and structure persuasion text.

In this section you will build on your existing knowledge of how persuasive writing works, thinking about its audience, purpose and form, and focusing on its typical structure and language features.

Audience, purpose, form

Persuasive writing puts forward a particular view and tries to get the reader to agree with that view. Some typical examples are:

- **adverts**, which try to persuade you to buy something
- **political speeches**, which try to persuade you to vote for or against a proposal
- **newspaper editorials**, which try to persuade you to agree with their point of view.

The audience for a piece of persuasive writing may not want to buy the product or agree with the view being expressed – that is why they have to be persuaded! Persuasive writing must be set out very clearly and attractively, and written in a forceful or clever manner in order to win over its audience.

TYPICAL FEATURES

The typical features of persuasion texts are listed below. You will need to refer to these in Section 2.

- The **audience** is someone whom you are trying to influence.
- The **purpose** is to change their view or to persuade them to do something.
- The **form** or structure that a persuasion text often takes is a series of points in a logical order, supporting a single viewpoint.

Typical **language features** of persuasion texts are:

- emotive[1] language, e.g. 'buy the books you **love**'
- personal language (use of first and second person), e.g. '**We** think **you'll** be impressed'
- weasel words[2]/phrases, e.g. 'So what's the catch?'

[1] **emotive** – designed to make the audience feel something
[2] **weasel words** – words that are deliberately misleading, meant to persuade someone to do or feel something

Task 1 — Reading and annotating

The start of the extract below has been annotated to illustrate all the language and the structural features of a persuasive text. Read the text and the annotations carefully, then annotate the second half to show where the same features occur.

A brilliant new way to buy the latest and best books.

Emotive language – designed to get you really interested

Structure – a series of points supporting one viewpoint

Just Good Books is a **brilliant** way to buy the books **you love** – and to discover new **favourites** too. As a member **we** will continue to offer **you** the latest and best books on a wide range of subjects – all at savings of up to 75% off the R.R.P. **We** think **you'll** be impressed by the choice **we** offer **you** and delighted by the low, low prices.

Personal pronouns – appealing directly to reader

Weasel words – words selected to deceive

So what's the catch? There isn't one!

All we ask is that, as a member, you buy just one more book from us in the next six months. One book, that's it! We're certain you'll want to buy more, but the choice is absolutely yours – we're that confident that you won't want to buy your books any other way!

No worries, we'll never send you a book you haven't ordered!

Once a month, we'll send you a free magazine featuring over 120 bestselling books. In the unlikely event you don't want to order anything, no worries, we won't send you anything you haven't ordered. We don't ask you to decline anything either, so there'll be no nasty surprises or unwanted packages on your doorstep.

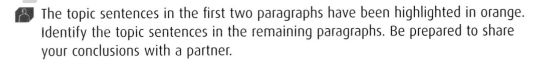

Just GOOD BOOKS *Just* pick up your phone now

Task 2 — Topic sentences

The topic sentences in the first two paragraphs have been highlighted in orange. Identify the topic sentences in the remaining paragraphs. Be prepared to share your conclusions with a partner.

Using text skeletons

In order to understand the structure of a text, it can be useful to draw a diagram or 'text skeleton'. Text skeletons represent the bare bones of a text.

The typical persuasion skeleton shows a series of main points listed down the page in a logical order, indicated by asterisks (✳). Each main point often has a paragraph to itself in the text. The labels to the left of the asterisks tell you the focus of each paragraph, for example '1. Book offer'. These labels are usually a shortened version of the topic sentence. The lines branching to the right from each asterisk summarise statements that back up or expand the main point, for example '75% off'. These are known as 'memory joggers'.

Using text skeletons will help you to analyse the structure of a text and plan your own writing.

Task 3 **Structuring**

Below is a half-completed text skeleton for the advertising flyer on page 75.
Complete the text skeleton so that you have a full set of notes on the text.

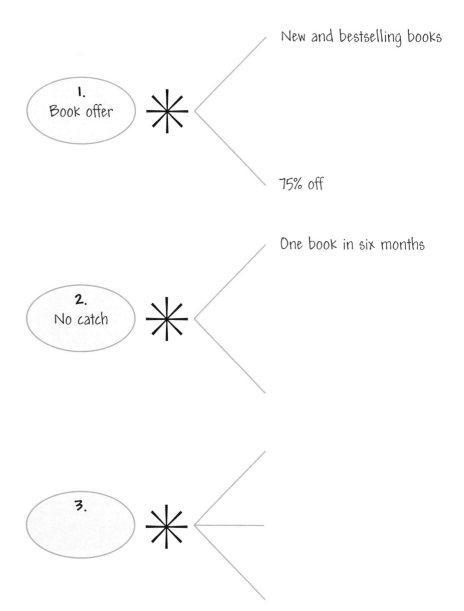

Composition and effect

AIMS

Identify the stylistic conventions of a persuasion text.

Show how the form and style of the text suits its audience and purpose.

Look in detail at the effect of the language choices made by the writer.

Write a short persuasive passage yourself in the same style.

In this section you will read a persuasion text and explore how it is effective. You will identify and discuss its key features, focusing on how it addresses its audience and the writer's choice of words and rhetorical devices.[1]

[1] **rhetorical devices** – techniques used to persuade an audience, such as alliteration (e.g. 'anywhere and anytime') and rhetorical questions (e.g. 'This is all about fun and wonder, remember?')

Test watch As well as building up your writing skills, the following sections are good preparation for the optional reading tests at the end of Year 7 because they help you to:

- comment on a writer's purpose and the effects of the text on the reader
- comment on the structure and organisation of texts
- comment on a writer's use of language
- deduce, infer or interpret information, events or ideas
- describe, select or retrieve information, events or ideas from texts.

If you show these skills in the reading test, you will gain a better mark.

Task 4 Reading

 The extract on pages 78–79 is from the home page of the Travelbak website. Travelbak is a company that sells trips into the future. As you read the extract, think about these questions:

- What is the purpose of this text?
- What features of the text tell you that it is a piece of persuasive writing?

Quote from an expert – backs up viewpoint

Emotive idea

Clever catchphrase

Introductory passage – grabs interest of the audience

Direct address – engages the audience

Weasel words – convince the audience

Emotive phrase – used to appeal to the dreams of the audience

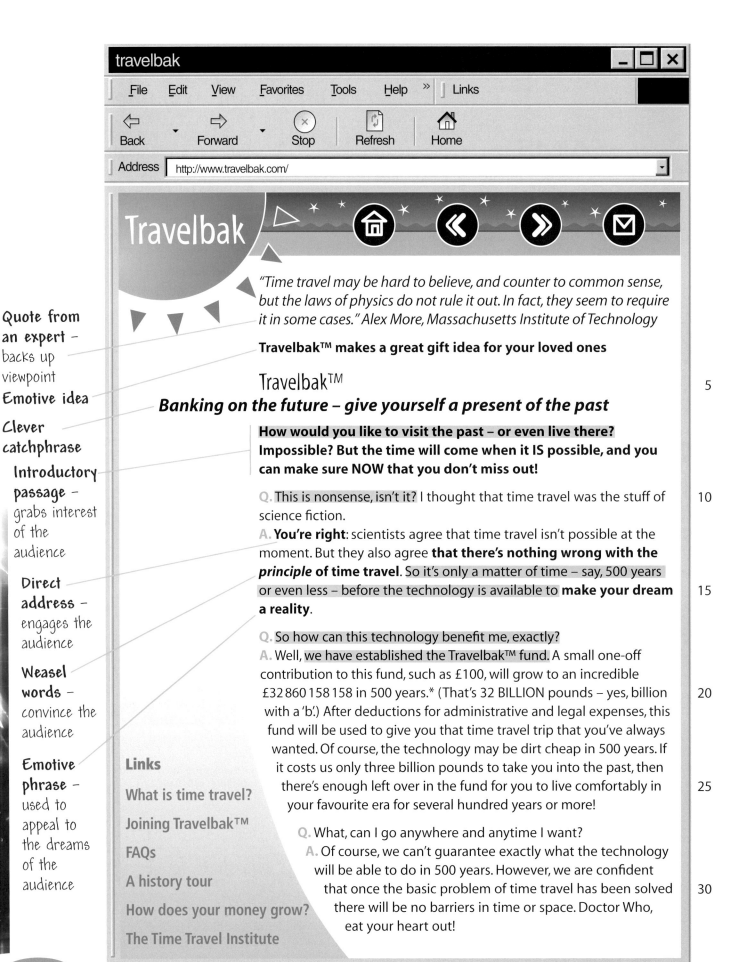

Travelbak

"Time travel may be hard to believe, and counter to common sense, but the laws of physics do not rule it out. In fact, they seem to require it in some cases." Alex More, Massachusetts Institute of Technology

Travelbak™ makes a great gift idea for your loved ones

Travelbak™
Banking on the future – give yourself a present of the past

How would you like to visit the past – or even live there? Impossible? But the time will come when it IS possible, and you can make sure NOW that you don't miss out!

Q. This is nonsense, isn't it? I thought that time travel was the stuff of science fiction.

A. **You're right**: scientists agree that time travel isn't possible at the moment. But they also agree **that there's nothing wrong with the *principle* of time travel**. So it's only a matter of time – say, 500 years or even less – before the technology is available to **make your dream a reality**.

Q. So how can this technology benefit me, exactly?

A. Well, we have established the Travelbak™ fund. A small one-off contribution to this fund, such as £100, will grow to an incredible £32 860 158 158 in 500 years.* (That's 32 BILLION pounds – yes, billion with a 'b'.) After deductions for administrative and legal expenses, this fund will be used to give you that time travel trip that you've always wanted. Of course, the technology may be dirt cheap in 500 years. If it costs us only three billion pounds to take you into the past, then there's enough left over in the fund for you to live comfortably in your favourite era for several hundred years or more!

Q. What, can I go anywhere and anytime I want?

A. Of course, we can't guarantee exactly what the technology will be able to do in 500 years. However, we are confident that once the basic problem of time travel has been solved there will be no barriers in time or space. Doctor Who, eat your heart out!

Links

What is time travel?

Joining Travelbak™

FAQs

A history tour

How does your money grow?

The Time Travel Institute

5

10

15

20

25

30

The Art of Persuasive Writing

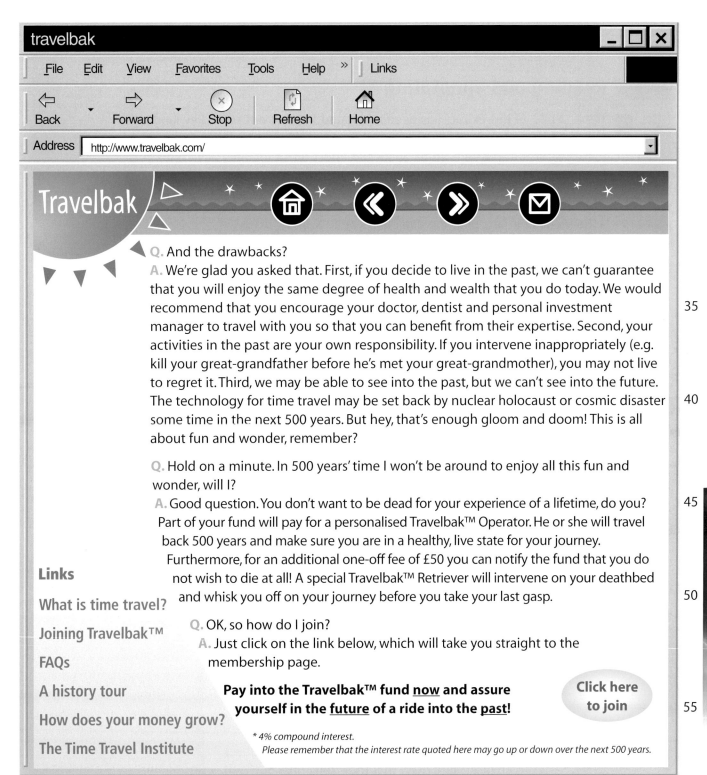

Q. And the drawbacks?

A. We're glad you asked that. First, if you decide to live in the past, we can't guarantee that you will enjoy the same degree of health and wealth that you do today. We would recommend that you encourage your doctor, dentist and personal investment manager to travel with you so that you can benefit from their expertise. Second, your activities in the past are your own responsibility. If you intervene inappropriately (e.g. kill your great-grandfather before he's met your great-grandmother), you may not live to regret it. Third, we may be able to see into the past, but we can't see into the future. The technology for time travel may be set back by nuclear holocaust or cosmic disaster some time in the next 500 years. But hey, that's enough gloom and doom! This is all about fun and wonder, remember?

Q. Hold on a minute. In 500 years' time I won't be around to enjoy all this fun and wonder, will I?

A. Good question. You don't want to be dead for your experience of a lifetime, do you? Part of your fund will pay for a personalised Travelbak™ Operator. He or she will travel back 500 years and make sure you are in a healthy, live state for your journey. Furthermore, for an additional one-off fee of £50 you can notify the fund that you do not wish to die at all! A special Travelbak™ Retriever will intervene on your deathbed and whisk you off on your journey before you take your last gasp.

Q. OK, so how do I join?

A. Just click on the link below, which will take you straight to the membership page.

Pay into the Travelbak™ fund <u>now</u> and assure yourself in the <u>future</u> of a ride into the <u>past</u>!

Click here to join

* 4% compound interest.
  Please remember that the interest rate quoted here may go up or down over the next 500 years.

Links

What is time travel?

Joining Travelbak™

FAQs

A history tour

How does your money grow?

The Time Travel Institute

Task 5 Topic sentences

Discuss what you think the purpose of this text is. Write this down in one sentence, and be prepared to share your sentence with the class.

Now consider what this text is about. The best way to do this is to look at the topic sentences, the first few of which have been highlighted in orange. Identify the remaining topic sentences. Be prepared to use these sentences to summarise the extract.

Features of a persuasive text

Task 6 ## Reading and annotating

 The first part of this extract has been annotated to bring out some key language features of a persuasive text. Annotate the rest of the text to illustrate as many of these features as possible. Think about the effect these features have once you have identified them.

You should consider the following questions in your discussion:

- How does the text grab the audience's attention?
- What is the main tense of the piece?
- How formal or informal is the language?
- Is the audience addressed directly?
- Are there any emotive or weasel words and phrases?

Make brief notes of your conclusions so that you can share them in a whole-class discussion.

Addressing the audience

The web page has been presented in a question-and-answer form. This means that the audience is reading what seems to be a real conversation between two people. Direct address (use of the second person, referring to 'you') is often used.

Task 7 ## Discussing

 Discuss the effect of a) the question-and-answer form, and b) direct address in persuasive writing. Note down three reasons why a writer of a persuasive text may wish to use these features.

To help you, here is a section of the text rewritten without using direct address.

> **Banking on the future – we make the past a present to our contributors**
> Now there is a chance to visit the past – or even live there. Impossible? But the time will come when it IS possible, and contributors to Travelback can make sure NOW that they don't miss out!

Powerful words to convince the reader

The words and phrases that a writer uses contribute greatly to the overall style and effect of the piece of writing. The style and effect of any piece of writing depends above all on the words and phrases that you choose. In persuasive writing in particular, you need to use powerful words to win over the audience.

Recording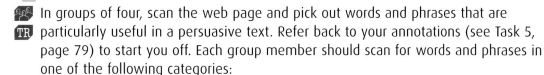

In groups of four, scan the web page and pick out words and phrases that are particularly useful in a persuasive text. Refer back to your annotations (see Task 5, page 79) to start you off. Each group member should scan for words and phrases in one of the following categories:

- **Emotive language** (value judgement words, strong and colourful words, weasel words), e.g. 'incredible', 'a small one-off contribution'.
- **Getting on the reader's side** (appearing reasonable, agreeing with the reader, showing a sense of humour), e.g. 'You're right', 'Good question'.
- **Clever language** (wordplay, slogans, invented words), e.g. 'a present of the past'.
- **Rhetorical devices** (repetition, alliteration, rhetorical questions), e.g. 'Anywhere and anytime'.

Select the two most effective examples that you have found in each category. Each group should be prepared to explain why they have selected their examples.

Making it persuasive

Task 9 **Writing**

Try to write a piece of persuasive text in the same style as the Travelbak text. You want to answer the question whether the Travelbak fund could allow people to travel into the future as well as the past. Here are some notes that you might make about this scenario.

> Can Travelbak allow people to travel into future?
> * The next 500 years look like the future to us.
> * But in 500 years' time they will be the past – so Travelbak can be used.
> * Clients' choice of time and place more risky – no one knows what will be happening where and when.
> * Extra payment as insurance against disaster could be made.

Discuss together how you could use these notes to help you write a paragraph of persuasive writing that could be included in the Travelbak web page. Remember that you need to:

- construct a logical argument – e.g. use logical connectives such as 'so' and 'but'
- address the audience directly – e.g. 'So you want to know...?' and 'You will be'
- include convincing words and phrases – e.g. 'the future is fab, too' and 'to put your mind at rest'.

Then work on your paragraph. You may like to begin in this way:

Q. Hey, what about travelling into the future – can I do that too?

The Art of Persuasive Writing

Text structure and organisation

Getting the structure right

AIMS

Analyse how the writer has organised the text by using a text skeleton.

Identify the signposts that the writer uses to make the text cohesive.

In this section you will use a text skeleton to help analyse the structure of the Travelbak web page. You will then think about what helps the text hang together. Finally, you will plan your own piece of writing.

Creating a text skeleton

Text skeletons sum up the structure of the text visually (see page 76). Using a text skeleton for a persuasion text will help you to understand the structure of the Travelbak web page.

Task 10 **Structuring**

  Look at the text skeleton and memory joggers for the beginning of the web page below. Complete the skeleton and memory joggers for the rest of the extract. You will find that the topic sentences that you identified in Task 5 (page 79) help you list the main points.

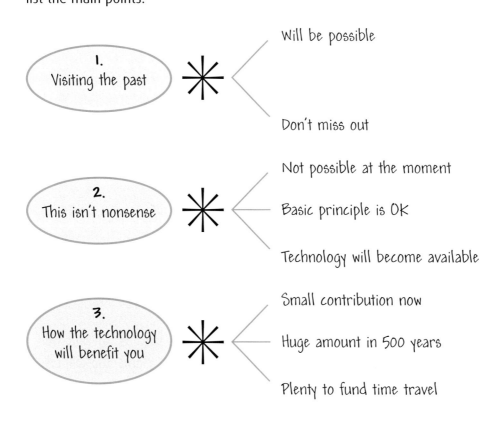

Discussing

 Discuss the following questions.

TR • The key points are presented in the form of questions and answers on the web page. How effective is this as a device to structure the text?

• Do the key points follow a particular order, or could they go in any order? Give your reasons.

• How do the arguments build up to convince the reader?

Signposting the text

Overall, the Travelpak text hangs together well. The paragraphs and question-and-answer format 'signpost' where the text is going.

But what about the individual sections of the text? Part of the persuasive writer's task is to connect and develop the argument by signposting it (making it cohesive) – see the explanation of cohesion on page 56. Clear signposting is also needed, therefore, within each paragraph to help the reader understand how ideas are connected and how the argument is developed.

GRAMMAR

- **Sentence connectives** – These show how a sentence is linked to the previous one, e.g. 'However', 'Quite apart from that'. **Conjunctions** are a type of sentence connective. They show how ideas are linked within a single sentence, e.g. 'although', 'but'.
- **Sentence signposts** – These include nouns or verbs, often at the beginning of a sentence, showing where a sentence is going, e.g. 'It is true that', 'Time travel is'.

Task 12 **Discussing**

 This section of text has had some of the signposting features highlighted. Discuss the purpose of each of the signposts, for example: '*So* links this sentence with...'

Then try to work out the colour coding.

Q. So how can this technology benefit me, exactly?
A. Well, we have established the Travelbak™ fund. A small one-off contribution to this fund, such as £100, will grow to an incredible £32 860 158,158 in 500 years. (That's 32 BILLION pounds – yes, billion with a 'b'). After deductions for administrative and legal expenses, this fund will be used to give you that time travel trip that you've always wanted. Of course, the technology may be dirt cheap in 500 years. If it costs us only 30 million pounds to take you into the past, then there's enough left over in the fund for you to live comfortably in your favourite era for several hundred years or more!

The Art of Persuasive Writing

Now look at the paragraph beginning with the question: 'And the drawbacks?' Try to identify as many signposting features as you can, and be prepared to explain how they work. Draw up a grid to record your ideas, like the one begun below.

Signposting feature	Type of signposting	How it works
And the drawbacks?	Conjunction	'And' links the sentence with the previous paragraph. Sometimes conjunctions begin sentences for effect.
We're glad	Sentence signpost	Shows where the sentence is going – it goes on to say what 'we're glad' about.

Letter to America

Task 14 Planning practice

 Your 12-year-old daughter is living with her aunt in America for a year. She has written asking you to contribute £100 to the Travelbak fund on her behalf. She won't talk to you directly about this. Plan a letter in reply, persuading her against being involved in such a scheme.

To help you, some abbreviated topic sentences are listed below, but they are in an illogical order. Rearrange them so that they could become a series of main points in a text skeleton for your letter. How do the signposts help you put them in a sensible order?

Anyway, I can't afford to waste £100

First, time travel is impossible

Second, Travelbak is a con

So I absolutely refuse to fund your scheme

But I worry about your state of mind

Finally, it is too dangerous

I was pleased to get your letter

However, I can't agree to you taking part in the scheme

Sentence structure and punctuation

Making the sentences work

AIMS

Use punctuation to clarify meaning, particularly between sentences and clauses.

Vary the structure, length and type of sentence within a paragraph to make writing more entertaining and effective.

In this section you will remind yourself of how punctuation can make your meaning clear. You will also explore how different kinds of sentence can be used to make a text interesting and persuasive.

Using punctuation for clarity

The main reason that we use punctuation in written texts is to make the meaning clear. In particular, punctuation shows:

- where one chunk of meaning ends and the next begins (e.g. a comma introduces a clause; a full stop indicates the end of a sentence)
- where there should be pauses of various kinds (e.g. full stops, commas and semicolons all indicate different lengths of pause)
- what kind of connection there is between different parts of a sentence (e.g. brackets, dashes and commas can mark off extra information in a sentence)
- the grammatical function of a clause or sentence (e.g. inverted commas show direct speech; a question mark indicates a question).

Task 15 **Reading and annotating**

 Reread the first question-and-answer section of the Travelbak web page (from 'Q. This is nonsense, isn't it?' to 'make your dream a reality'). Identify each punctuation mark and explain why it has been used.

Variety is the spice of persuasion

If your sentences all sound or look the same, your writing will be dull! There are many ways in which you can vary your sentences to keep your reader interested. You can:

- vary the **length** of your sentences from short to medium to long
- vary the **type** of your sentences using simple, compound, complex
- vary the **tone** of your sentences so they are both formal and informal.

Task 16 **Discussing**

 Look at the following section of the Travelbak web page. It has been annotated to show the different kinds of sentence that have been used. Discuss these, giving two or three examples of how they make the text:

- focused
- entertaining
- effective.

The Art of Persuasive Writing

Short punchy sentence to begin

Rhetorical question; second person; light tone

Long sentence to end – a complex sentence of two main clauses followed by a subordinate clause

A. **Good question.** You don't want to be dead for your experience of a lifetime, do you? Part of your fund will pay for a personalised Travelbak™ Operator. He or she will travel back 500 years and make sure you are in a healthy, live state for your journey. Furthermore, for an additional one-off fee of £50 you can notify the fund that you do not wish to die at all! A special Travelbak™ Retriever will intervene on your deathbed and whisk you off on your journey before you take your last gasp.

Simple sentence; third person; formal, serious tone

Compound sentence

Complex sentence – also an **exclamation**

Task 17   Writing

 Imagine that you would like the law to be changed to prevent companies such as Travelbak from making money out of people. Write a short letter to your MP to persuade him or her to raise the issue in Parliament. You should focus on making the structure and length of your sentences as varied as possible. Try to include several of the following:

- a short, simple sentence, e.g. 'The practice must stop.'
- a compound sentence, e.g. one that combines main clauses with 'and' or 'but'
- a complex sentence, e.g. one with a subordinate clause beginning 'which'
- a question or exclamation, e.g. 'Do you agree?' or 'It is appalling!'
- a variety of tones, e.g. formal to show that you are serious and informal for a special effect.

Here is the beginning of one such letter. Complete the letter by adding at least five sentences.

Ms Mina Armitage MP
House of Commons
London W1

21 November 2005

Dear _____

Are you aware of the threat that firms such as Travelbak represent to the public?

5) Composing a persuasive letter

AIMS

Plan, draft and revise a persuasive text with reader and purpose in mind.

Organise ideas into a coherent sequence of paragraphs.

Vary your sentence structure and length to lend pace, variety and emphasis.

Your task

Write a persuasive letter. First revisit how to lay out a letter. Then plan, draft and revise your writing to make it as persuasive as possible.

Test watch This writing task is good preparation for the type of writing required in your English tests because it helps you learn how to:

plan your work so that it is organised logically into well-constructed paragraphs that are linked together well

compose your writing effectively to match its audience and purpose,

and select powerful vocabulary

vary the structure of your sentences and punctuate them correctly.

If you show these skills in the optional English test at the end of Year 7, you will gain a better mark.

1 Audience and purpose

This continues Task 14 on page 84.

Your 12-year-old daughter is living with her aunt in America for a year. She has written asking you to contribute £100 to the Travelbak fund on her behalf. She won't talk to you directly about this. Your task is to plan a letter in reply, persuading her against being involved in such a scheme.

Discuss what effect the audience and purpose of this letter will have on the style. In particular, consider:

Will the letter be informal, formal, or a mixture of the two?

What sort of tone might you use as a parent?

It is very important for you to get your message across to your daughter. How will this affect the language and style of the letter?

2 Brainstorming the content

In groups of four, brainstorm the main arguments that you could use to persuade your daughter against getting involved in the fund. Try to come up with six points, but don't get

sidetracked into the detail of the arguments at this stage. The planning practice that you did on page 84 will give you some ideas to build on.

The Art of Persuasive Writing

3 Planning the structure

 The form of this piece of writing will be a letter rather than a question-and-answer. Remind yourself of the layout of an informal letter:

Your address here

The date

Informal greeting (e.g. 'Dear Sarah,')

Main text of the letter, divided into paragraphs for structure.

Informal ending, e.g. 'Your loving father'

Signature of writer

Now think about the structure of the main text of your letter. As this is a piece of persuasive writing, you should use the persuasion text skeleton (see page 82) to structure it.

4 Creating a text skeleton

 Choose three of the key points from your brainstorming session and arrange them in a logical order on a text skeleton.

Your first paragraph could be an introduction, which gives your first reactions to your daughter's letter and states firmly that you cannot agree to her request.

The next paragraphs would give the main reasons. You could end with your most important point to give maximum effect.

A concluding paragraph could sum up the main points or provide a final blow to your daughter's plans.

Look back at the 'Planning practice' on page 84 to see how you structured the letter. Can you improve on that structure here?

Finally, develop each point by adding one or two memory joggers. Your skeleton could begin like this:

Thanks for your letter

1.
Introduction

Travelbak is a bad idea

The Art of Persuasive Writing

Composing your piece

Now add some flesh to the text skeleton by drafting your persuasive letter.

Points to remember

As you write, remember to:

- make your letter as persuasive as possible. Use emotive language, rhetorical devices and appeal to the audience – your daughter (see page 85)

- signpost your argument by using sentence connectives and other means to give direction and structure to the paragraphs (see page 83)

- vary the length and type of your sentences to make the writing as powerful as you can (see page 85).

You may want to use some of the sentence signposts and connectives given below to help you.

Sentence signposts and connectives

- How could you possibly
- Think how dangerous
- First
- Finally
- Quite apart from that
- Time travel is

- Do you really think
- Their extraordinary idea
- Second
- Anyway
- It worries me that

- Throwing money away
- However
- Third
- And there's another thing
- I know that you

 # Peer comment

Swap your draft with your partner's and read each other's carefully. Discuss what works well and highlight this on the drafts. Then discuss how you could improve particular sections. Jot down your suggestions on the draft.

Redraft parts of your persuasive letter where necessary, using your partner's comments to guide you.

Pulling it all together

  Listen to extracts from letters written by members of your class.

 Decide what are the key features that make these extracts effective. Be prepared to feed your ideas back to the class.

Set up to three targets for yourself for improving your next piece of persuasive writing.

How argument text works

AIMS

Revisit the key ingredients of an argument text.

Use text skeletons to help analyse and structure an argument text.

In this section you will build on your knowledge of how to present an argument, thinking about its audience, purpose and form, and focusing on its typical structure and language features.

Audience, purpose, form

Argument text is any text that uses a structured, logical argument to express a point of view. Examples are:

- **letters to newspapers**, such as arguing that Britain shouldn't go to war
- **business proposals**, such as arguing that the business should open another branch
- **newspaper and magazine articles** that give the point of view of the writer.

Arguing a case is a particular kind of persuasion. In argument texts, some of the ingredients of persuasive writing (see pages 74–89) are more important than others.

TYPICAL FEATURES

The typical features of argument texts are listed below. You will need to refer to these in Section 2.

- The **audience** is someone you are trying to influence.
- The **purpose** is to get them to agree with your argument.
- The **form** or structure that an argument text often takes is a series of points in a logical order, supported by evidence giving a single viewpoint. It should begin with an opening statement and end with a conclusion.

Typical **language features** of argument texts are that:

- the language should be **formal** and **impersonal**, e.g. avoiding colloquialisms,[1] e.g. 'Even government ministers admit that the prison system is failing.'
- the **third person** is generally used instead of directly addressing the reader, e.g. 'they may well'
- the tone should be **reasonable** and **restrained** – you want to win over your audience by reason more than with too many emotive words or clever rhetorical devices[2], e.g. 'Isn't it meant to be the other way round?'

[1] **colloquialism** – the kind of language used in conversation. It often includes slang and dialect, e.g. 'Doing time doesn't work'

[2] **rhetorical devices** – techniques used to persuade an audience, such as alliteration ('anywhere and anytime') and rhetorical questions ('This is all about fun and wonder, remember?')

Read the magazine article below, which argues that the prison system is not working. One example of each of the elements listed has been highlighted. Identify at least two other places where each element is used by the writer.

Talk about the effect of these features.

DOING TIME DOESN'T WORK

If it's broke – fix it

Clear opening statement

Formal and impersonal language

Prison does not work – official. Even government ministers admit that the prison system is failing. If the hospitals or any other public service performed as badly there would be a
5 national outcry. **But somehow prisoners are 'out of sight, out of mind'**. Prisons are in crisis: **they are bursting at the seams, riots occur almost every month, and the suicide rate is at record levels**.

And what do MPs – our official representatives – plan to do about it? Well, nothing. You would think that MPs care about
10 one of the most serious problems confronting society and would want to ask the government a few questions, like: why is it that we are sending more and more criminals to prison, when statistics show that people are more likely to commit further offences if they are sent to jail? **Isn't it meant to be**
15 **the other way round?**

Rhetorical device

So why have recent prison laws – at least one in each year since Tony Blair became Prime Minister – made prison sentences even longer and tougher? Only because a lot of voters think that tougher sentences are a deterrent.[1] But
20 tougher sentences are not a deterrent. They may well deter those who are frightened by a spell in prison, but the prison population is made up of the poorest or least educated people. To these people, the thought of 'doing time'
25 is not such a big deal.

Third person

Restrained language and reasonable tone

Evidence – supporting the opening statement

The Art of Presenting an Argument

91

Besides, sending offenders to prison has the opposite effect to that which is intended. Latest figures – again the Prison Service's own figures – show that 56 per cent of criminals who were sent to prison committed another crime within two years. That's a disgraceful record. In contrast, well under half of criminals who were given community sentences[2] offended again within a two-year period.

So let us listen to reason rather than to emotion. Violent offenders, who are a real threat to public safety, clearly need to be locked up. For the majority, however, community sentences make more sense. Apart from being more caring and more effective, they allow offenders to give something back to society. They are also cheaper. Harry Fletcher, assistant general secretary of the probation[3] union NAPO, believes that community sentences cost the taxpayer a tenth of what it costs to keep somebody in prison for the same period.

Doing time does not work – official. It's time that our official representatives woke up to this fact, and acted on it.

[1]**deterrent** – if the thought of going to prison stops you committing a crime, then prison is a deterrent

[2]**community sentence** – when the offender spends his sentence working for the community rather than in prison

[3]**probation** – probation officers supervise and help offenders

Task 2 Topic sentences

Discuss what you think the purpose of this text is. Write this down as one sentence, and be prepared to share your sentence with the class.

Now consider what this text is about. The best way to do this is to look at the topic sentences – the first two of which have been highlighted in orange. Identify the remaining topic sentences. Be prepared to use the sentences to summarise the extract for the rest of the class.

Using text skeletons

In order to understand the structure of a text, it can be useful to draw a diagram or 'text skeleton' to show its bare bones.

As you read the article you may have noticed how its structure is summed up by the persuade text skeleton (see page 76). The asterisks are the main points of the argument, which are often a shortened form of the topic sentences. The memory joggers are the supporting statements that back up or expand the main point.

Using text skeletons will help you to analyse the structure of a text and plan your own writing.

Task 3 **Structuring**

Below is a half-completed text skeleton for *Doing Time Doesn't Work*. Complete the skeleton and memory joggers so that you have a full set of notes on the text and a clear picture of its structure.

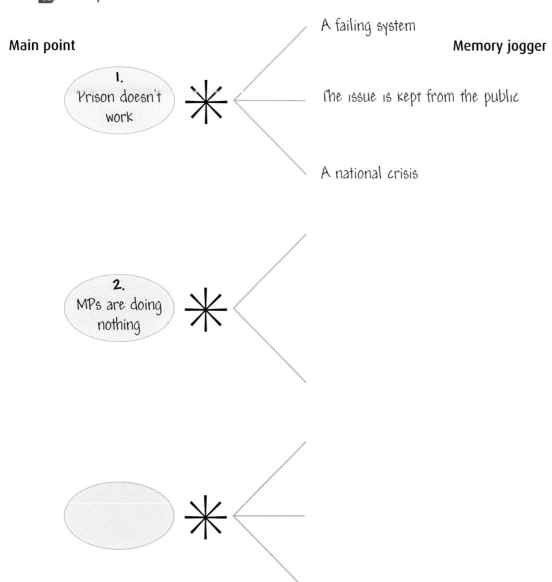

Main point

Memory jogger

1. Prison doesn't work

A failing system

The issue is kept from the public

A national crisis

2. MPs are doing nothing

Composition and effect

AIMS

Identify the stylistic conventions of an argument text.

Discover how the writers of non-fiction use language and style to good effect.

Find and use different ways to strengthen an argument.

In this section you will explore in more detail how the article *Doing Time Doesn't Work* is effective. You will focus first on how it uses formal language and different kinds of questions. Then you will identify several ways of backing up your argument, and practise using these techniques.

Test watch As well as building up your writing skills, the following sections are good preparation for the optional reading tests at the end of Year 7 because they help you to:

- comment on a writer's purpose and the effects of the text on the reader
- comment on the structure and organisation of texts
- comment on a writer's use of language
- deduce, infer or interpret information, events or ideas
- describe, select or retrieve information, events or ideas from texts.

If you show these skills in the reading test, you will gain a better mark.

Making questions work for you

Questions can be very useful tools for writers of persuasive and argument texts. They can be used:

- to vary the tone, so it isn't just factual statements or opinions
- to raise an issue that will be answered later in the piece
- to emphasise a point by turning it into a question and answer
- for dramatic or persuasive effect (a **rhetorical question**[1]).

> [1] **rhetorical question** – question that doesn't need answering, e.g. 'Are we going to give up?'

Task 4 Discussing

 Four questions have been used in the article *Doing Time Doesn't Work*. Identify the questions and discuss which of the tasks listed above they are doing. How effective are these questions? Be prepared to share your conclusions.

Keeping it formal

Most arguments – especially if they concern a serious issue – need to be written using Standard English.[1] In Section 1 you identified some formal features of the language used in *Doing Time Doesn't Work*. You are now going to look at formal language more closely.

[1] **Standard English** – the language used by most educated writers of English, for example in newspapers, textbooks and speeches in debates

Task 5 — Analysing language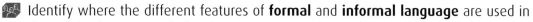

Identify where the different features of **formal** and **informal language** are used in the article. (One example has been given in each case.) Try to find two more of each (not all will have two examples). Draw up a grid to record your ideas.

Formal	Examples	Informal	Examples
More complex/ compound sentences	'Even government ministers admit'	Mainly simple sentences	'Prison does not work'
Impersonal	'Latest figures show'	Direct address	'You would think that'?
The passive	'prison population is made up of'	Contractions	'doesn't'
Spelling out phrases in full	'does not'	Slang/colloquialisms	'doing time'
Use of Standard English	'Even government ministers'	Dialect words/fillers	'Well'
Includes specialist/ difficult vocabulary	'public service'	Mainly straightforward vocabulary	'prison does not work'

Now discuss the questions:

- What is the balance of formal to informal language in the article?
- Why has the writer used informal language, and how effective is it?
- Why do argument texts mainly rely on formal language?

Creating a CLEVER argument

The purpose of an argument is to persuade the reader or audience to accept your point of view. There are several techniques that you can use to strengthen your argument:

- **Criticise** the opposing view (e.g. 'Some people say…but')
- **List** factual or statistical evidence (e.g. 'The facts show that')
- Provide **Examples** of what you mean (e.g. 'Cats, for example,)
- Quote or refer to someone's **Views** (e.g. 'The manager agrees that')
- Refer to your own or others' **Experience** (e.g. 'When I was a boy')
- Give logical **Reasons** (e.g. 'because').

> The word 'CLEVER' will help you remember these techniques:
> **C**riticise
> **L**ist
> **E**xamples
> **V**iews
> **E**xperience
> **R**easons

Remember: a CLEVER argument is a strong argument!

Task 6 Recording

Scan the article *Doing Time Doesn't Work* for examples of 'CLEVER' techniques.
Draw up a grid to classify them.

Technique	Examples
Criticise	'Only because a lot of voters think...'
List	'they are bursting at the seams'

Choose the most effective technique that the writer uses to strengthen the
argument that prisons don't work.

Task 7 Writing

Compose six different ways of backing up a different argument:

X 'Young people, not old people, are most likely to be victims of crime.'

TR In each case use only one or two sentences. Focus on the CLEVER techniques. (Note:
You can make up any facts, statistics, comments or events to support your argument.
Some ideas are provided below, along with some possible sentence signposts.)

Young women are next most at risk of attack

One in five young men under 24 years old suffered a violent attack in 2001

Parents are still allowed to smack children

Mobile phone theft is huge

More children than teachers get bullied at school

One in four teenagers in Bolton was a victim of crime in 2002

Young people face a far higher risk of violence than the elderly, according to the British Crime Survey

'The most likely victim of a theft, assault, wounding, robbery, a sexual offence and homicide is a young person' (NSPCC website)

Sentence signposts and connectives

- **CRITICISING** THE OPPOSING VIEW
  Opponents say...but
  It is ridiculous to claim that

- **LISTING** FACTUAL OR STATISTICAL EVIDENCE
  The evidence is clear
  Just look at the facts

- PROVIDING AN **EXAMPLE** OF WHAT YOU MEAN
  For example,
  In practice, this means that

- QUOTING OR REFERRING TO SOMEONE'S **VIEWS**
  I am not alone in thinking
  To quote the prime minister himself

- REFERRING TO YOUR OWN OR OTHERS' **EXPERIENCE**
  I saw three girls the other day
  As my friend, Rob, will agree

- GIVING A LOGICAL **REASON**
  The reason for this is obvious
  It clearly follows that

Text structure and organisation

AIMS

Identify the purpose and effectiveness of the opening and closing paragraphs of a text.

Use a text skeleton to help analyse and structure an argument text.

In this section you are going to look at how important beginnings and endings are in making an argument structured and effective. Then you will plan and end an article yourself.

Beginnings

 Task 8 **Discussing**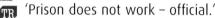

The article *Doing Time Doesn't Work* begins with the statement:
'Prison does not work – official.'

- Discuss how effective you think this is as the opening sentence of an argument. To help, you may like to compare the following possible openings:
  - Prison doesn't work.
  - Even according to official statistics, prison doesn't work.
  - I want to argue in this article that prisons don't work.
  - The other day I was talking to a prisoner, let's call him Brian, who has spent the last 23 years in jail.

Endings

Endings are important, too. An ending has to make as much of an impact on the reader as the beginning, leaving them with a clear idea of the argument that you are making. An ending also rounds off the argument, often by referring to the beginning, so that the piece hangs together as a satisfying whole.

Here are some different ways in which you can make an ending effective, together with possible paragraph openings:

Type of ending	Possible paragraph openings
Summarise your main points	'To sum up' 'To conclude'
Restate the main issue, with a punchy response	'The question was' 'So we are now in no doubt'
Make a final, knockout argument which leaves the reader in no doubt as to the rightness of the case	'One final point' 'The most important point of all, however,'
Return to the example, character, anecdote or theme of the opening, adding a comment or completing the story in some way	'Perhaps Mr X should have thought about these issues before he...'

The Art of Presenting an Argument

Discussing

Reread the final paragraph of *Doing Time Doesn't Work* on page 92. Discuss whether the writer has used one or more of these ending techniques. How effective do you find this ending?

Task 10 **Planning practice**

A newspaper editor has given you the opening paragraph of an editorial about young people and drug-taking. She has also left you with a few notes about some of the reasons behind young people taking drugs. Plan the rest of the article.

The harsh facts behind drug-taking

The Home Secretary yesterday stated that young people turn to drugs because they have nothing better to do. Nothing could be further than the truth. The reasons behind the vast increase in drug taking among young people are many and complex, but boredom comes low on the list.

Reasons behind drug-taking
* curiosity – experimenting
* to feel grown up/independent/different
* escape from personal problems
* peer pressure
* feel less anxious
* increase/reduce energy levels
* lots of pushers

Use a persuade text skeleton to select at least four of the bullet points above as the main points in your argument. Then add one or two memory joggers to develop or expand each main point. For example, you could begin your skeleton like this:

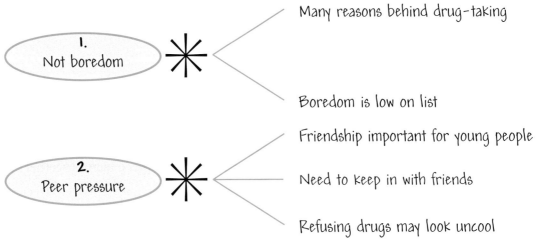

Task 11 **Writing**

The editor liked your structure and used it to write most of the article. She left the final paragraph for you to complete. Write an effective concluding paragraph. Remember:

- Think of the type of ending that you want (see the table on page 97).
- Open your paragraph in an effective way to show that you are rounding off the argument.
- You may want to refer to the editor's opening paragraph above, or to the main points and memory joggers in your skeleton.
- Swap your final paragraph with a partner's and comment on each other's writing. Can you suggest any ways in which your partner can make their ending more effective?

Sentence structure and punctuation

Making the sentences work

AIMS

Revisit the passive voice and understand when it is effective to use it.

Recognise how varying the length of sentences gives writing rhythm, impact and interest.

In this section you will revisit the effective use of the passive. You will also experiment with making your sentences more interesting by varying their length.

Using the passive

GRAMMAR

Active versus passive

- In an **active sentence**, the subject of the sentence is the 'agent' of the action (verb) and the object of the sentence is acted upon by the subject:
  'The policeman arrested the burglar.'

- In a **passive sentence**, the subject of the sentence is acted upon by the verb. The agent is added after the verb and introduced with 'by':
  'The burglar was arrested by the policeman.'

- Often the agent is omitted altogether from passive sentences:
  'Twenty-seven people were arrested.'

Subject

Object

Object

Object

Verb

Agent

Verb

Verb

Passive sentences are less common than active, and you must use them with care. However, in some circumstances they can be very useful, for example:

- when the doer of the action is unknown
- when you want the focus of the sentence to be on the thing being acted on
- when you want the writing to be more formal, impersonal and general.

Task 12 **Passive**

Look at lines 16–42 of the article *Doing Time Doesn't Work* and identify the passive sentences. Why has the writer used the passive in each of these cases?

Task 13 **Active**

Rewrite these sentences to make them more effective by replacing the underlined active clauses with the passive. (Note: You may have to alter the wording slightly.)

1 The Home Secretary has suggested that <u>judges should give people a five-year minimum sentence for carrying an illegal gun</u>.

The Home Secretary has suggested that people carrying an illegal gun should be given a five-year minimum sentence.

2 He was speaking after a New Year shooting in Birmingham when <u>some gunmen killed two teenagers in a shoot-out</u>.

3 <u>In fact guns are responsible for only 0.12 murders per 100 000 people in Britain.</u>

4 <u>Many politicians also criticised violent gangster rap music</u>.

Giving your sentences rhythm

To keep the reader's interest while you try to win them over to your point of view, you will need to vary the length of your sentences, giving them a more interesting rhythm.

Task 14 **Discussing**

 Reread *Doing Time Doesn't Work* and discuss the rhythm of the sentences in lines 43–45. In particular, consider these questions:

- Which sentences are short? Which are medium in length? Which are long?
- Why are the sentences not all the same length?
- How effective is this particular rhythm?
- Which is the sentence with the most impact?
- What gives it this impact, and why has the writer used it in this way?

Task 15 **Writing**

 Read the extract from the article *Today's Prisons* below, which argues that the prison regime has the right balance of harshness and humanity.

> Prisons throughout history have been harsh, grim places. Today's prisons still have quite strict regimes. Prisoners have little privacy and no freedom. There are many restrictions on their life. That is the price of their crime. However, modern prisons are not meant to be simply places of punishment. For example, they encourage people to study. Outsiders and visitors are also allowed to come in. Writers take creative writing classes. The idea is to give the prisoners skills and knowledge. When they are released they are more likely to get a career. They are also less likely to end up in prison again.

- Rewrite the extract, making some sentences longer than others. You can do this by:
  - combining sentences by using conjunctions (e.g. 'and', 'but', 'although')
  - using punctuation to break up sentences or combine clauses (e.g. colons and semicolons)
  - leaving one or two short sentences for effect
  - altering individual words to fit your new structure.

 Swap your version with your partner's. Is their version more effective than the original text?

5 Composing your own argument

AIMS

- Plan, draft and revise an editorial with reader and purpose in mind.

- Organise ideas into a coherent sequence of paragraphs, opening and closing the piece appropriately.

- Vary your sentence length to lend pace, variety and emphasis.

- Use different ways to validate your argument.

Your task

Write a newspaper editorial with a strong argument, using all the aspects of good argumentative writing highlighted in this unit.

Test watch This writing task is good preparation for the type of writing required in your English tests because it helps you learn how to:

plan your work so that it is organised logically into well-constructed paragraphs which are linked together well

compose your writing effectively to match its audience and purpose and

select powerful vocabulary

vary the structure of your sentences and punctuate them correctly.

If you show these skills in the optional English test at the end of Year 7, you will gain a better mark.

---

1 Audience and purpose

Imagine that a notorious child-killer, Maia Shipley, is about to be released from prison after serving 35 years of a life sentence. Now aged 53 she is a reformed character and is training to be a priest. It is your job to write a short editorial for a broadsheet newspaper,[1] either in favour of or against her early release.

Discuss what effect the audience and purpose of this editorial will have on the style of the article. In particular, consider these questions:

Will the language be informal, formal or a mixture of the two?

How will you help the reader to follow the argument?

[1] **broadsheet newspaper** – a larger format newspaper

2 Brainstorming the content

First decide whether you want to argue for or against the decision to release Shipley. Choose three or four main points that you want to make, then team up with someone who has chosen

the same argument and brainstorm the main points to back up your view. Don't get sidetracked into the detail of the arguments at this stage.

To help you, some pointers for possible arguments have been provided beneath the newspaper headlines below.

KEEP SHIPLEY IN JAIL

Murder is a terrible crime

A life sentence should mean a life behind bars

We need to set an example to others

SHIPLEY HAS DONE HER TIME

She is a reformed character

Prison is a waste of time and money in her case

She will do society more good out of prison

3 Planning the structure

Now think about the structure of your editorial. Your arguments will provide the key points of the structure. Put the arguments in a sensible order, and use the persuade skeleton to think about how you would develop each one. For example:

Training for priesthood

1. Reformed character

Doctors say she is sane

Experience has changed her life

Now think about your remaining paragraphs and add your ideas to the skeleton plan.

4 Composing your piece

Now you are ready to add some flesh to the text skeleton by drafting your editorial.

Points to remember

As you write, remember to:

- use formal English, including the passives where appropriate (see pages 94 and 99)
- vary the length of your sentences for effect (see page 100)
- include some questions for variety or rhetorical effect (see page 95)
- use the CLEVER technique to make your arguments strong (see page 95)
- open the piece by grabbing the reader's interest and clearly stating your position, and end the piece effectively (see page 97).

You may want to use some of the sentence signposts and connectives below to help you.

Sentence signposts and connectives	
• Some people say	• Therefore
• Her work as a priest shows	• Because
• Many criminals are reformed	• So
• The Home Secretary himself	• But
• Imagine what the victims' parents feel	• However

5 Peer comment

 Swap your draft with a partner's and evaluate how effective their editorial is. Does it present a persuasive argument? Discuss what works well and highlight this on the draft. Then discuss how you could improve particular sections. Jot down your suggestions on the draft.

Use the feedback to write up a final version for the newspaper.

6 Pulling it all together

  Listen to extracts from the editorials written by members of your class.

With a partner, decide on the key features that make these extracts effective. Be prepared to feed your ideas back to the class.

Set up to three targets for yourself for improving your next piece of argument writing.

H The Art of Writing Advice

1 How advice text works

AIMS

Explore the key ingredients of advice text.

In this section you will learn about texts that give advice, thinking about their audience, purpose and form, and focusing on their typical structure and language features.

Audience, purpose, form

Texts that give advice come in many forms. Books, leaflets and magazine articles provide advice on everything from keeping fit to dealing with teenagers or looking after a rabbit. The audience is the person who is seeking advice, for example someone who wants to know how to cope with noisy neighbours.

When you give advice, you are often combining several text types:

- **Persuasion**, persuading the reader to act in a particular way
- **Argument**, giving reasons why the advice is good
- **Information**, providing facts which support the advice
- **Instruction**, telling the reader about how to do something.

The techniques of persuasion and argument are particularly useful, however (see pages 74-103).

Read the following extract from an advice book aimed at young teenagers. One example of each of the language and structural features has been highlighted.

Identify at least two other places where each feature is used by the writer. Think about the effect of these features once you have identified them.

Note: The two sentences highlighted in orange are topic sentences. You will return to these in Section 2.

How to Handle Your Younger Sister or Brother

Subheading – indicates a new section

Second person – makes the advice personal

Sentence signpost – flags an important point

The problem…

Everything was fine until they came along. **You were just getting the hang of this** parent/child relationship thing when **out pops 'Junior' and screws everything up. Great!**

Little brothers and sisters…aren't they sweet – NOT! **The thing is**, although they tend to be smaller and weedier, the option to pummel them until they shut hup is not a good one. **You can guarantee tat no matter how weak they claim you've left them,** they'll always have enough strength left to crawl to your mum and dad, and enough breath left in them to splutter…' It was your other child who did this to me!' The only thing for it is to bite your lip when they're stressing you out. Instead of ignoring them, shouting at them or hitting them, get them on your side – believe it or not they can come in useful for all sorts of things.

Conversational tone – with slang terms

5

Reason given for the previous point

10

15

Tell me about it

'My sister will go on and on until you kick her, then when she's sure there's something to see she rushes off screaming to my mum to show her.'

Philippa, 14

What they'll come in useful for...

- *Fetching and carrying your things*, e.g. drinks, snacks, your shoes, magazines. Basically, if you've got them trained correctly, you can send them off hunting for anything that isn't within easy reach. 20

- *Being used as decoys to distract your parents*. If you want to get everyone off your case, send in Junior to entertain and keep everyone occupied while you go about your business. 25

- *Sharing a laugh with when your mates aren't around*. Yes, believe it or not, if you make the effort to spend some time with the little sprog, you may discover that he/she actually possesses something like a sense of humour. 30

How to handle them...

It's all about patience. If you can take a deep breath and count to ten silently while they're winding you up, you can then take the more mature approach to this older/younger sibling arrangement. Make the most of the fact that somewhere deep inside them they probably look up to you and, in many ways, admire you. Use this admiration sensibly and you may find yourself with a helpful little ally. 35 40

From *A Survivor's Guide to Families* by J Baker
(published by Hodder and Stoughton Ltd)

Task 2 Feedback

Share the features you indentified with the class.

Write down two features of advice texts that are shared by persuade texts and two features that are different. You may want to check the features of persuade texts on page 74.

The Art of Writing Advice

Composition and effect

AIMS

To take the reader of an advice text into account when phrasing advice.

To use an appropriate level of formality when addressing a particular readership.

In this section you will consider how to make an advice text suit its purpose and audience, focusing on phrasing the advice and adopting an informal, friendly style.

Test watch As well as building up your writing skills, the following sections are good preparation for the optional reading tests at the end of Year 7 because they help you to:

- comment on a writer's purpose and the effects of the text on the reader

- comment on the structure and organisation of texts

- comment on a writer's use of language

- deduce, infer or interpret information, events or ideas

- describe, select or retrieve information, events or ideas from texts.

If you show these skills in the reading test, you will gain a better mark.

Purpose and content

Task 3 Feedback

 Look back at the extract *How to Handle Your Younger Sister or Brother* on pages 105–106. Discuss what you think the purpose of this text is. Write this down as one sentence, and be prepared to share your sentence with the class.

Now consider what this text is about. Look at the topic sentences, the first two of which have been highlighted in orange. Identify the remaining topic sentences. Be prepared to use these sentences to summarise the extract for the rest of the class.

Softening up commands

Advice texts often include instructions as they help the reader to do something or act in a certain way. In straightforward instruction text, such as a recipe, the imperative[1] is used. For example: '*Add* 500g of flour' (see also page 69).

To get the reader on their side, writers of advice texts can soften their commands. Instead of beginning a sentence with the command 'Sit down', for example, you could:

- use a question, e.g. 'Would you sit down?' 'Why don't you sit down?'

- make the command conditional (add 'if') or hypothetical (add 'could'), e.g. 'If you sit down, you will…', 'You could sit down'.

[1]**imperative** – a sentence or clause that gives an instruction, e.g. 'Go away!' or 'Sit down', is an imperative. Imperatives are also known as directives or commands.

The Art of Writing Advice

107

Writing

Try softening up some commands yourself. The following sentences advise teenagers on how to deal with family rows, but they have all used the imperative. Rewrite them to make them gentler and more effective, and try to use a different method in each case.

1 Think before you scream.

2 Choose your moment before you raise a controversial issue.

3 Know when to compromise.

4 Learn to listen to the other side of the argument.

Writing informally

Another way to get the reader on your side is to make sure that the advice is written in a friendly, informal tone. Remind yourself of the features of informal writing (see page 94).

Writing

The extract below is advice addressed to teenagers about keeping their room tidy. Your challenge is to use the techniques of informal writing to make the advice more suitable to a younger teenage audience.

Read the extract and discuss what you would need to change before you start writing your own version. Consider using the following techniques:

- Use shorter sentences, without so many subordinate clauses, e.g. the first sentence could end with the word 'hotel'.
- Use direct address, e.g. 'you' instead of 'teenagers'.
- Use more colloquial language, e.g. 'your mum' instead of 'their mother'.
- Contract common phrases, e.g. 'It's hardly fair' instead of 'It is hardly fair'.
- Add humour, e.g. 'If you insist on covering every square inch of floor space with rubbish...'
- Use more straightforward vocabulary, e.g. 'brothers and sisters' instead of 'siblings'.

> Teenagers should remember that they are not living in a hotel; there is no maid who comes round every morning to clean and tidy their room. If their room remains messy, their mother will almost certainly feel obliged to do this for them, and the only way to prevent such an intrusion is for them to tidy it themselves.
>
> It is hardly fair for teenagers to say that, as it is their room, they can keep it as dirty and messy as they please. Certain standards have to be maintained, and their parents and siblings should not have to tolerate such mess in their midst.

Text structure and organisation

AIMS

Use a text skeleton to help analyse and structure an advice text.

Use bullet points to identify and elaborate points and help the reader navigate the text.

In this section you will investigate the overall structure of an advice text, and practise using bullet points to structure your advice in a clear and elegant way.

Using a text skeleton

It is important to structure advice clearly so that the reader can understand and follow it. This can be achieved using a diagram or text skeleton to show its bare bones. Using text skeletons will help you to analyse the structure of a text and plan your own writing.

As you read the extract *How to Handle Your Younger Brother or Sister*, you may have noticed how its structure is summed up by the persuade text skeleton (below). The asterisks are the main points of the advice, which are often a shortened form of the topic sentences. The memory joggers are the supporting statements that back up or expand the main point.

Task 6 | **Text skeleton**

Below is the beginning of a text skeleton for the extract. Complete the skeleton so that you have a full set of notes on the text and a clear picture of its structure.

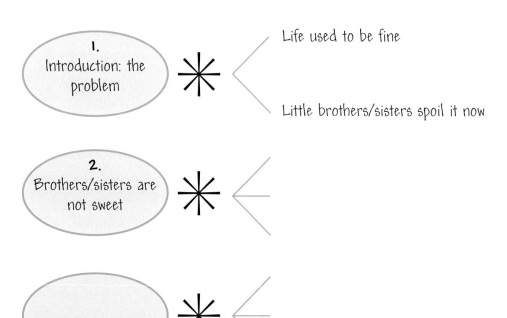

Look back at the extract. How does the way the text is presented visually help the reader?

Developing bullet points

Bullet points are a useful, punchy way to present advice. They don't have to form complete sentences but often consist only of a key phrase or clause, which may then be followed by an example or reason to back it up.

 Task 7 **Discuss**

Look at the section of the advice text starting 'What they'll come in useful for' (page 106, lines 19–32). Discuss the features that make this section hang together so that it is easy for the reader to find their way around. In particular, think about these questions:

- Which presentational features are repeated in this section?
- What forms of words are repeated in this section?
- Why do you think the writer has used these patterns?

See the explanantion of coherence and cohesion on page 56.

 Task 8 **Writing**

The extract below, which is part of a different advice text, also contains some bullet points.

Extend each bullet point with a sentence or two, giving an example or a reason, in the way that the writer of the extract on brothers and sisters has done:

- What do you notice about how each bullet point begins?
- Why do you think the writer has repeated this pattern?

> ## Manners do matter
> - You should treat others as you would like them to treat you.
> - You should try to be respectful of others' feelings, needs and customs.
> - You should take time to be courteous and polite.

 Task 9 **Planning practice**

Imagine that the section 'Manners do matter' is the first part of a short advice text on how to do well in your first job. The text skeleton for this section would look like this:

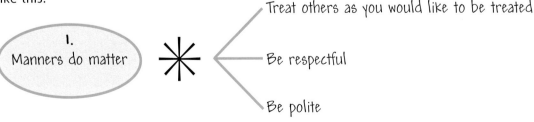

Plan the rest of the advice text in a similar way, using a text skeleton. Some of the topics you may like to cover are: clothes, tidiness, timekeeping, hard work and working with others. Try to plan at least two further sections.

Making the sentences work

AIMS

Explore the use and structure of conditional sentences, and use punctuation to clarify their meaning.

Make your writing more interesting by combining simple sentences into compound and complex sentences.

In this section you will explore how complex sentences can make your writing more interesting, including conditional sentences.

Conditional sentences

Each of the three bullet points in the advice text on page 106 was followed by a sentence beginning with the conjunction 'if'. For example: 'Basically, if you've got them trained correctly, you can send them off hunting for anything that isn't within easy reach.'

This kind of complex sentence is called a conditional sentence.

GRAMMAR

A **conditional sentence** tells you that if one thing happens, another thing will (or could) follow. In other words, that thing will follow **on condition that** the first thing happens.

- The subordinate clause (the 'if' clause, or the 'conditional' clause) tells you the condition.
- The main clause tells you what will or could happen if the condition is met.

For example:

Conditional clause ──── If you've got them trained correctly, | you can send them off hunting for anything that isn't within easy reach. ──── Main clause

The conditional clause doesn't have to come first in the sentence, for example:

Main clause ──── You can send them off hunting for anything | if you've got them trained correctly. ──── Conditional clause

The negative of a conditional clause can be expressed in two ways:

- If...not
- Unless

For example:

- <u>If you haven't</u> got them trained correctly, <u>you can't</u> send them off hunting for anything that isn't within easy reach.
- <u>Unless</u> you've got them trained correctly, <u>you can't</u> send them off hunting for anything that isn't within easy reach.

Note: When the subordinate clause comes first in the sentence, it is important to mark the division between the two clauses with a comma.

The Art of Writing Advice

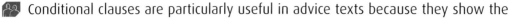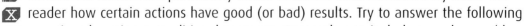
Conditional clauses are particularly useful in advice texts because they show the reader how certain actions have good (or bad) results. Try to answer the following questions by using a conditional sentence. Remember to include two clauses (the conditional clause and the main clause) and to use punctuation where necessary. (Note: The first one has been done for you.)

1 What will you do if your friend asks you out tonight? (Begin with 'If')

If he asks me out tonight, I will certainly say 'Yes'.

2 What will you do if your mum wants you to stay in instead? (Begin with 'If')

3 Will you have a row if she wants you to do your homework? (Begin with 'We')

4 What do you think will happen if you have a row? (Begin with 'If')

5 What will be the result if you don't control your temper? (Begin with 'Unless')

6 What would happen if you buttered your mum up first? (Begin with 'She')

Making your sentences more interesting

Task 11 **Discuss**

Look at the following two versions and discuss which one is more effective. Be prepared to give your reasons.

The thing is, although they tend to be smaller and weedier, the option to pummel them until they shut up is not a good one. You can guarantee that, no matter how weak they claim you've left them, they'll always have enough strength left to crawl to your mum and dad, and enough breath left in them to splutter, 'It was your other child who did this to me!'

They tend to be smaller and weedier. You have the option to pummel them until they shut up. But this option is not a good one. You may leave them very weak. But they will always have enough strength left to crawl to your mum and dad. And they will have enough breath left in them too. They will splutter, 'It was your other child. He did this to me!'

The writer of the first version has used only two sentences, and yet the meaning is quite clear. It is also much more interesting than a string of short, simple sentences. She has managed to do this by using **complex sentences**.[1] (See also page 18.)

[1]**complex sentences** – sentences with main clauses, subordinate and coordinate clauses

It is now your turn to write more interesting sentences. How many different ways can you link the following two simple sentences to form one complex sentence?

Mum was late back from work.
She was in a bad mood.

You will need to use some **conjunctions** to link them. To make a compound sentence you will need a **coordinating conjunction**, and to make a complex sentence you will usually need a **subordinating conjunction**.

For example:

Mum was late back from work, <u>and</u> she was in a bad mood. — Coordinating conjunction

or

<u>When</u> Mum was late back from work, she was in a bad mood. — Subordinating conjunction

(Note: You can play with the order of the clauses and alter the wording slightly. Remember to indicate the boundaries of the clauses by using punctuation correctly.)

- Try to write six different sentences using the two simple sentences as ingredients.

GRAMMAR

Conjunctions are words that join different parts of sentences and show the relationship between one clause and another.

Coordinating conjunctions join two main clauses to make a compound sentence. These are the main coordinating conjunctions:

- and
- but
- for
- yet
- so

Subordinating conjunctions join a subordinate clause to a main clause to make a complex sentence. These are the main subordinating conjunctions:

- when
- whenever
- while
- as soon as
- although
- since
- because

The Art of Writing Advice

AIMS

- Plan, draft and write a piece of informal advice, anticipating the needs, interests and views of the audience.

Your task

Write a self-help pamphlet/leaflet on family life, focusing on all the aspects of good advice writing highlighted in this unit.

Test watch This writing task is good preparation for the type of writing required in your English tests because it helps you learn how to:

- plan your work so that it is organised logically into well-constructed paragraphs which are linked together well

- compose your writing effectively to match its audience and purpose and

- select powerful vocabulary

- vary the structure of your sentences and punctuate them correctly.

If you show these skills in the optional English test at the end of Year 7, you will gain a better mark.

1 Audience and purpose

 You are writing a self-help pamphlet aimed at young teenagers, and you have reached the section called *Managing Your Mum and Dad*. What advice do you want to give your audience on how to manage their parents?

Discuss how the purpose and audience of this text will affect its style. In particular, consider:

- the tone that you will adopt. Will it be humorous, like the extract 'How to handle your younger sister or brother', or more serious?

- the kind of language that you will use.

2 Brainstorming the content

Think of three or four main points of advice that you want to make and brainstorm possible ideas. Will you deal with Mum and Dad separately or together? Think about:

- How to deal with arguments, such as disputes over clothes or tidying your room.

- How to get round them when you want something, such as a loan or a lift somewhere.

- How to cope with their embarrassing habits, such as their terrible jokes.

- How to enjoy their company, such as while watching TV or on family holidays.

3 Planning the structure

 Now think about the structure of your section. Your main points of advice will provide the key parts of the structure.

Put them in a sensible order and they will become the backbone of your text skeleton (the asterisks).

Then consider how you would develop each point. Add memory joggers to the skeleton which:

> give a reason why the advice should be followed, or
>
> give an example of what you could do, or
>
> give an example of what could happen if you don't.

Now think about your opening and closing paragraphs and add your ideas to the skeleton plan. They need not be long but bear in mind:

> the opening needs to grab the readers' interest as well as state clearly the purpose of the section
>
> the conclusion should sum up the advice in a punchy fashion.

Composing your piece

 You are now ready to begin writing.

Points to remember

As you write, remember to:

- address the advice to the reader, using the second person, but phrase any instructions carefully, softening commands (see page 107)
- use a conversational tone and informal language, while not departing too much from Standard English because you are writing a pamphlet (see page 108)
- give reasons why your advice should be followed
- present your advice clearly, perhaps including bullet points (see page 110)
- try to use complex sentences for effect, including conditional sentences and a range of subordinating and coordinating conjunctions (see page 111).

You may want to use some of the sentence signposts and connectives below to help you.

> **Sentence signposts and connectives**
>
> - Dealing with arguments
> - How to get round your parents
> - You know how embarrassing
> - If you...then
> - The reason for this is simple
> - Maybe you should
> - When you are on holiday
> - Unless you...you won't

Peer comment

 Swap your draft with your partner's and evaluate how effective the advice is, highlighting what works well on the draft. Then discuss what you need to do to improve particular sections and jot down your suggestions.

Use your partner's feedback to write up a final version of your advice text. Include some presentational features to make the section attractive and its structure clear to the reader.

Pulling it all together

 Listen to extracts from the advice written by members of your class.

 With a partner, decide on the key features that make these extracts effective.

Set up to three targets for yourself for improving your next piece of advice writing.

I The Art of Discursive Writing

 **How discursive text works**

AIMS

- Revisit the key ingredients of discursive text.
- Use text skeletons to help analyse and structure discursive text.

In this section you will build on your existing knowledge of how a discursive text works, thinking about its audience, purpose and form, and focusing on its typical structure and language features.

Audience, purpose, form

Discursive (or discussion) writing is used when you want to present arguments and information from different points of view. Some typical examples are:

- **broadsheet newspaper[1] articles** covering controversial issues, e.g. whether fox-hunting should be banned
- **student essays** in subjects such as English and history, e.g. 'Was America right to invade Iraq?'

The audience for discursive writing is someone who wants to make up his or her mind about an issue by reading or listening to the evidence and arguments on both sides.

[1] **broadsheet newspaper** – a larger format newspaper

TYPICAL FEATURES

The typical features of discursive text are listed below. You will need to refer to these in Section 2.

- The **audience** is someone who is interested in an issue.
- The **purpose** is to help someone understand the issue by presenting the arguments as fairly as possible.
- The **form** or structure is often a series of paragraphs, each presenting a different point, in a logical order, beginning with an introduction and ending with a reasoned conclusion.

Typical **language features** of discursive texts are:

- present tense and third person, e.g. 'Time raises many basic questions'
- formal and impersonal language, e.g. 'On the one hand are the scientists'
- logical connectives signposting stages in the argument, e.g. 'however'
- sentence connectives showing whose point of view is being discussed, e.g. 'On the other hand are the religious fundamentalists'

Reading and annotating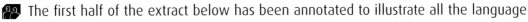

The first half of the extract below has been annotated to illustrate all the language and structural features of a discussion text. Read the text and the annotations carefully, then annotate the second half to show where the same elements occur.

Why has the past tense also been used in this passage?

Present tense

Logical connective

What is Time?

Time **raises** many basic questions about the nature of life. **As** the Bible states, 'There is a time to be born and a time to die.' But what is time itself? **The concept of time has concerned people of all cultures for as long as human beings have existed.**

Formal and impersonal language

Structure
– series of contrasting points

Theories about time tend to fall into two camps. **On the one hand** are the scientists who try to make sense of the world around them, looking for evidence to back up their ideas. On the other hand are the religious fundamentalists of a whole range of faiths, who seek explanations for the world and all its works in the holy book of their particular religion.

Sentence connective –
showing point of view

For example, in the late Middle Ages, Christian scholars tried to work out from the Bible how many years had passed between the making of Adam and the birth of Christ. They concluded that God had begun the six-day creation of the Earth on 23 October 4004BC. This led to precise dates being added in the margins of the Old Testament.

In the late eighteenth century, however, William Smith's investigations into the geology of the British Isles made him realise that some rocks were very old indeed, possibly stretching back millions of years before Christ. His theories were dismissed by a society not open to new ideas.

Task 2 **Topic sentences**

The topic sentences in the first two paragraphs have been highlighted in orange.

Identify the topic sentences in the remaining paragraphs to help you summarise its content. Be prepared to share your conclusions.

The Art of Discursive Writing

Using text skeletons

In order to understand the structure of a text, it can be useful to draw a diagram or 'text skeleton'. Text skeletons represent the bare bones of a text.

The typical discursive skeleton shows a series of points (asterisks) moving down the page in a logical order. Each major point has a contrasting view in the opposite column. You could think of the two columns as the points 'For' and 'Against' a particular view.

The main points of a discursive text are generally backed up by examples, argument or evidence before the opposing point is made. These supporting statements can be added as lines to the skeleton so that you have a complete set of memory joggers.

                                          *   *
                                          *   *
                                          *   *

Using text skeletons will help you to analyse the structure of a text and plan your own writing.

Task 3   Structuring

Below is a half-completed text skeleton and memory joggers for the discursive text *What is Time?* (Note the numbers that show the path of the argument in the text.)

Complete the text skeleton and memory joggers so that you have a full set of notes on the text and a clear picture of its structure.

1. Introduction to issue of time	
Viewpoint	**Opposite viewpoint**

Memory jogger

2. Scientists try to make sense of world — Look for evidence to back up ideas

3. Religious fundamentalists have different view — Look to holy books to explain the world

Main point

2 Composition and effect

Learning from example

AIMS

- Identify the stylistic conventions of a discursive text.
- Show how the language and organisation of the text suits its purpose.
- Look in detail at how the writer distinguishes the different views expressed.
- Comment on the effectiveness of the ending and write an ending presenting a different point of view.

In this section you will read a discursive text and explore how it is effective, focusing on its language, the way it is organised and the way it ends.

Test watch As well as building up your writing skills, the following sections are good preparation for the optional reading tests at the end of Year 7 because they help you to:

- comment on a writer's purpose and the effect of the text on the reader
- comment on the structure and organisation of texts
- comment on a writer's use of language
- deduce, infer or interpret information, events or ideas
- describe, select or retrieve information, events or ideas from texts.

If you show these skills in the reading test, you will gain a better mark.

Task 4 **Reading and discussing**

Read the piece of discursive writing below carefully, then discuss the following questions:

- What do you think is the purpose of the text? Write this down as one sentence.
- What do you think makes it effective? Name at least two things. Be prepared to share your thoughts.

How Did Time Begin?

How did time, life and the universe begin? This is a big question – indeed, it is one of the biggest that has ever been asked. **Many different and conflicting answers have been offered, but** perhaps **the most dramatic conflict is** the one fought out by the creationists (who believe God created the universe) and the scientists (who believe it was created in a 'Big Bang').

Present tense and third person

5

Formal and impersonal language

Logical connective

The Art of Discursive Writing

119

Sentence signpost
– introducing a
point of view

Sentence signpost
– introducing a
point of view

According to creationist Christians, God created the sun and stars and planets, **as well** as all the kinds of animals that ever lived, including humans. **Some creationists believe** that the universe was made less than 10 000 years ago; **other creationists believe** that it is billions of years old. The important point is that it was created by God. **The evidence for this view** is in the Bible, which states, 'In the beginning God created the heavens and the earth' (Genesis 1:1).

Sentence signpost –
introducing
point of view

Sentence signpost –
reinforcing a
point

According to most scientists, however, time and the universe were born in a gigantic explosion about 15 billion years ago – the so-called Big Bang. The universe rapidly expanded from this fireball, then slowly condensed into galaxies[1]; here, eventually life evolved from single-celled organisms. There are three main pieces of evidence for the Big Bang theory. Firstly, the universe is still expanding today, as a result of the original explosion. Secondly, astronomers have found traces of the explosion in the universe. Finally, the huge amount of certain chemicals in the universe, such as hydrogen and helium, is explained by the hot, dense period that followed the Big Bang.

The creationists claim that they are not anti-science. On the contrary, they say that the Big Bang theory itself is unscientific, and breaks some of the most basic laws of science. For example, the total amount of energy in the universe should always be the same. Yet before the Big Bang there was apparently no energy at all! The scientists admit that the Big Bang doesn't follow the usual laws of physics, but they argue that in extreme conditions physics does not follow the usual laws.

We are all familiar with the idea of 'cause and effect': something happens (X) because of something else (Y), which itself must be caused by something else (Z) and so on. The creationists say that if you go back to the start of the chain of cause and effect, there must be a 'first cause', which can only be God. So there must have been something that caused the Big Bang; it could not have happened out of nothing. But that is exactly what the scientists claim – that there was, literally, *nothing* before the Big Bang. This was when time and space were actually born.

50 Creationists also point to the wonderful patterns and beauty of life in the world, and argue that this could not have happened by accident and for no reason. God, therefore, must have created the universe. Scientists also find patterns in the world; they call them natural laws, however, and are quite happy to leave it at that. The

55 laws have their own slow working out (called evolution): they do not need a Grand Lawmaker.

Finally, creationists believe in the literal[2] truth of the Bible, and nothing will shake that belief. If the Bible says that the world was created by God in six days, then that is exactly

60 how it happened. Scientists prefer to believe in the evidence around them, rather than the words of an ancient, though sacred, book. Besides, they say, the creation story in Genesis should be taken as a myth – a story with its own 'poetic' truth – rather than as literal fact.

65 In conclusion, it seems as if scientists and creationists come from different planets themselves, as they hold such different views about the origins of time and the universe. I admire the strong religious belief of the creationists; in the end, however, their arguments rely on

70 the flimsy evidence of the Bible. As the scientists say, the Bible should not necessarily be taken literally anyway. The views of the scientists are preferable, as they are base on observation, not faith. Although it is an extraordinary theory, the Big Bang does seem to fit the

75 facts. It is a big answer to a very big question.

---

[1] **condensed into galaxies** – took the form of stars
[2] **literal** – taking the words as factually true

Features of a discursive text

Task 5 **Reading and annotating**

The first part of *How Did Time Begin?* has been annotated to bring out some of the key language features of a discursive text. Annotate the rest of the text to illustrate as many of these features as possible. Think about the effect of these features once you have identified them. (Look back at page 116 to remind you of the language features of discursive texts.) Note: Topic sentences have been highlighted in orange for the first two paragraphs. You will need to return to these in Section 3.

Now answer the following questions:

- The present tense is used in general, but the past tense also occurs. Why?
- The piece is written in the third person, apart from one place in the last paragraph where the first person is used. Why is the first person used here?

Making the viewpoint clear

Reading and discussing

 When different views are being discussed, it is important for the audience to know who holds which view. Look carefully at paragraph 4 of *How Did Time Begin?* (see below). The annotations show how the first four sentences make it very clear:

- who holds the view
- what the view is and how this relates to the overall argument. Discuss how the colour coding helps to bring out these features of the writing.

Sentence signpost – noun and verb introduce the main point

Sentence connective – indicating opposition

> The creationists claim that they are not anti-science. On the contrary, they say that the Big Bang theory itself is unscientific, as it breaks some of the most basic laws of science. For example, the total amount of energy in the universe should always be the same. Yet before the Big Bang there was apparently no energy at all! The scientists admit that the Big Bang doesn't follow the usual laws of physics, but they argue that in extreme conditions physics does not follow the usual laws.

The view

Sentence signpost – pronoun and verb introduce a supporting point

Supporting point – with extended example

Notice how the following features make the viewpoint very clear:

- The group with the particular point of view is identified early in the sentence or clause (e.g. the noun 'creationists').
- The verb then introduces the main point that the group is making (e.g. 'claim that...'). Together these form a sentence signpost.
- The point of view itself is then given (e.g. 'the Big Bang theory itself is...').
- If the point needs to be extended in some way, a pronoun[1] is used to remind the reader who holds the view, and a verb is used to introduce the supporting point (e.g. 'they say that...').

 Look at the final sentence in the extract above and discuss how it could be annotated to show how its features make the viewpoint clear.

[1] **pronoun** – a word used to replace a noun or noun phrase, e.g. 'I', 'he', 'that', 'which'

The Art of Discursive Writing

Coming off the fence

Discursive texts mainly present different points of view in a fair and balanced way. At the end of the essay or article, however, the writer usually states which argument they think is more convincing. The conclusion of a discursive text, therefore, often consists of the following features:

- A **summary** of the main arguments or a statement summing up the kind of debate that has been outlined

- A statement of the **personal view** of the writer, backing one or other of the views discussed and **giving reasons**

- A **final sentence** or two to round off the piece, perhaps by referring to the title of the piece or the introduction.

Task 7   Discussing

Look at the final paragraph of *How Did Time Begin?* and discuss whether these ingredients are present. How effective are they?

Task 8   Writing

Write a completely different conclusion to this piece. Imagine that you think the creationist view is more convincing – how could you conclude the piece most effectively? You may like to structure your conclusion like this:

Summary	The creationists provide four main arguments to back up their claim that God, not the Big Bang, created time, life and the universe. In brief, these are
Statement of personal view, with reasons	Their arguments seem to me to be convincing. In particular,
Final sentence or two to round off	The question was 'How did time begin?'

> There are many different verbs that give viewpoints. You don't have to use 'say' or 'think' all the time. Use some of these in your conclusion:
> - claim
> - believe
> - admit
> - argue
> - deny

Scan the essay *How Did Time Begin?* on pages 119–121 for other 'viewpoint' verbs.

3 Text structure and organisation

Getting the structure right

AIMS

- Analyse different ways in which a writer can organise discursive text by using a text skeleton.

- Identify the topic sentence in a paragraph and understand how this helps to orientate the reader.

In this section you will use a text skeleton to analyse the structure of 'How Did Time Begin?' You will also explore how a writer can organise and connect supporting and opposing points to make a discursive text clear and coherent.

Task 9 ## Topic sentences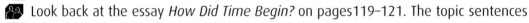

Look back at the essay *How Did Time Begin?* on pages 119–121. The topic sentences for the first two paragraphs have been highlighted in orange. Identify the topic sentences in the rest of the extract and the key points that follow them.

Task 10 ## Structuring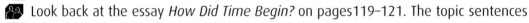

Imagine that a children's magazine called *Time and Space* wants to publish an article based on *How Did Time Begin?* As an editor on the magazine, your job is to break up the text and make its meaning clear for younger readers by adding subheadings to each paragraph. You have five minutes to reread the text and add the subheadings before the magazine goes to print.

The first subheading has added to start you off. (Note: The first paragraph does not need a subheading as it comes immediately after the main heading.)

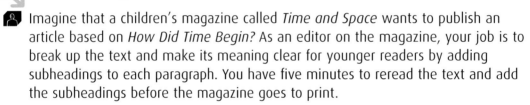

What creationists believe
According to creationist Christians, God created the sun and stars and planets, as well as all the kinds of animals that ever lived, including humans.

When you have finished, share your subheadings in small groups and discuss these questions:

- How similar are all your subheadings?
- How similar are they to the topic sentences in each paragraph?
- What does this tell you about the job that the topic sentence does in a paragraph?

Analysing the structure

Task 11 **Structuring**

Sketch a discursive text skeleton, like the one begun below, to sum up the structure of the essay *How Did Time Begin?* The topic sentences that you identified in Task 9 will help you to sum up the main points of each paragraph. Then add memory joggers to give the supporting points.

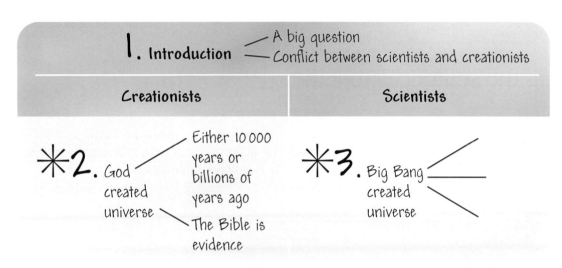

1. Introduction — A big question
— Conflict between scientists and creationists

Creationists	Scientists

*2. God created universe
— Either 10 000 years or billions of years ago
— The Bible is evidence

*3. Big Bang created universe

Task 12 **Planning practice**

Plan a discursive essay with the title *Are Humans Masters of the Universe?* Below are the topics of each paragraph, arranged in a random order. Your task is to rearrange the topics so that they form a series of main contrasting points in a text skeleton for your essay.

* * * * * *

A Humans can defeat diseases and improve quality of life

B Conclusion: Summary of arguments and personal opinion

C There are no higher life forms than humans

D Scientific achievements make humans the masters

E There may be higher life forms on other planets

F Science brings us nuclear weapons and GM crops

G Introduction: Are humans masters of the universe? Or are they less powerful than they think?

H There will always be diseases and viruses that will beat us

Share your essay structure with the class.

The Art of Discursive Writing

Making the sentences work

AIMS

- Identify how connectives help to organise sentences in a paragraph so that they relate to the main point and to each other.

In this section you will explore how different types of connectives make the links between your sentences clear.

Linking the sentences together

In a clear piece of writing, the main point of the paragraph is often in the opening sentence. But how does the writer link the remaining sentences in the paragraph to this main point, and to each other, so that the line of the discussion is clear? The main sentence structure tool is the **connective**. (Using connectives helps make a text cohesive – see the explanation on page 56.)

Task 13 **Discussing**

 Two particularly useful kinds of connective in discursive texts are connectives of **addition** and **opposition**. Read the extract below and discuss the purpose of the connectives. Which colour highlights connectives of addition and which highlights the connectives of opposition? (Note: The topic sentence is highlighted in orange.)

> The creationists claim that they are not anti-science. On the contrary, they say that the Big Bang theory itself is unscientific, and breaks some of the most basic laws of science. For example, the total amount of energy in the universe should always be the same. Yet before the Big Bang there was apparently no energy at all! The scientists admit that the Big Bang doesn't follow the usual laws of physics, but they argue that in extreme conditions physics does not follow the usual laws.

— Topic sentence

GRAMMAR

Connectives of addition allow the writer to **add** examples, evidence or supporting points when presenting a view. For example:

- and
- in addition,
- as well as
- for example
- another feature is

Connectives of opposition allow the writer to bring in a different or **opposing** point of view, or to qualify[1] what has just been said. For example:

- but
- however,
- on the other hand
- yet
- others object that

Note: Connectives can be used at the beginning of sentences (sentence connectives) or at the beginning of phrases or clauses within a sentence.

[1] **qualify** – you qualify a statement by adding a detail to make it less strong, e.g. 'I really liked the film, *but it went on too long.*'

Task 14 ## Writing

Use some connectives in your writing. Here are some unconnected statements about the end of the world:

> - A disease like AIDS may infect increasing numbers of people.
> - The Earth may gradually overheat, making life impossible.
> - God may bring the world to an end and judge evildoers.
> - There are so many nuclear weapons that soon they may be used in anger and devastate the Earth.
> - A comet or planet may collide with the Earth.

The task for each of you is to combine the statements so that they make one continuous paragraph. One of you should write under the heading 'The pessimists' view of the future'. As all the statements above are pessimistic, you should use mainly **connectives of addition**. You could begin your piece:

Pessimists believe that the world faces a frightening future. For example...

The other should write a single paragraph under the heading 'How will the world end?' You are presenting opposing views, so you should use mainly **connectives of opposition**. You could begin:

There are many conflicting theories about the end of the world. Some people...

You will probably need to alter the order or the wording of the sentences at times, especially when using connectives of opposition.

- When you have finished, swap your paragraphs and give your partner some critical feedback. Have they made good use of connectives to structure the sentences and link them together?

AIMS

- Plan, draft and revise a discursive essay, using a text skeleton to structure your writing.

- Organise your ideas into coherent paragraphs, using the first sentence of each paragraph to indicate the topic, and introduce and conclude the piece effectively.

Your task

Plan, draft and write a discursive text for a magazine, concentrating on all the skills learned so far.

Test watch This writing task is good preparation for the type of writing required in your English tests because it helps you learn how to:

plan your work so that it is organised logically into well-constructed paragraphs that are linked together effectively

compose your writing effectively to match its audience and purpose,

and select powerful vocabulary

vary the structure of your sentences and punctuate them correctly.

If you show these skills in the optional English test at the end of Year 7, you will gain a better mark.

1 Audience and purpose

Your challenge is to write a discursive piece for your school magazine entitled *Does Humankind Have a Future?* The piece will discuss the question seriously, looking at two main points of view:

pessimists who believe the world will end fairly soon, and

optimists who believe we have several million years left on the planet at least.

Discuss what effect the audience and purpose of the text will have on the style. In particular, think about these questions:

Will the language be formal and impersonal or informal and personal?

How will you signpost to the reader which view you are following at any particular point?

Brainstorming the content

First brainstorm ideas on both sides of the argument. Bearing the discursive text skeleton in mind, you will find it useful to divide a piece of paper into two columns and jot the arguments down in the left- or the right-hand columns, depending on which point of view the arguments support. For example:

Does humankind have a future?

No (the pessimists)	Yes (the optimists)
A disease like AIDS will eventually wipe out humans	Scientists have always managed to come up with cures and solutions
Global warming will make life impossible	Humans are masters of the environment

Try to think of three or four arguments for each point of view.

Planning the structure

Choose the arguments that you want to use and arrange them in a logical order on a text skeleton. If you can organise your points so that they 'answer' each other (as in the example above), the structure of your discussion will be similar to that of *How Did Time Begin?* Each paragraph will tackle a particular point (e.g. diseases), and include the arguments for and against that point. (See Diagram a).

If, however, your arguments do not link neatly to each other, you can use a simpler model. You could give all the views of one side (e.g. the optimists) first before moving on to the other side (the pessimists). (See Diagram b).

Now that you have identified your main points, try to expand the arguments by giving examples, or by pointing out their drawbacks. Add these supporting points to your plan in the form of memory joggers. For example, your first point may look like this:

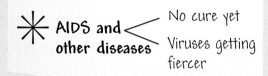

Don't forget to include an introduction and a conclusion to your plan. As this will be a short piece (no more than 400 words), you should use your introduction to give a very brief preview of each side in the discussion. For example:

How long have we got on the planet? Pessimists look to the future with fear and anxiety: they think that the end of time is not too distant. Optimists, however,...

Diagram a

Introduction	
No	Yes
1. - - - - ➤	2.
3. - - - - ➤	4.

Diagram b

Introduction	
No	Yes
1.	3.
2. ▼	4. ▼

Composing your piece

 Now begin the actual writing.

Points to remember

As you write, remember to:

- write in the present tense, unless you are describing things that happened in the past or that will happen in the future (see page 121)
- use formal language and the third person
- distinguish the different views by indicating clearly who holds the views and by using pronouns (see page 122)

- identify the main point of each paragraph by using topic sentences (see page 117)
- link the remaining sentences clearly by using sentence signposts and connectives, especially of addition and opposition (see page 126)
- make sure your punctuation is clear and accurate
- end by summing up the arguments and giving your own view (see page 123).

You may want to use some of the sentence signposts and connectives below to help you.

Sentence signposts and connectives

- Some people say
- The pessimists, however
- Optimists point to
- The growth of nuclear weapons
- What about advances in technology?
- In conclusion
- So who is right?

- In addition
- Furthermore
- To back this up
- Whereas
- However.
- Countering that view
- Disease is still a huge problem

Brainstorming the content

Swap your draft with your partner's and read each other's carefully. Discuss what works well and highlight this on the drafts. Then discuss how you could improve particular sections. Jot down your suggestions on the draft.

Redraft your article where necessary, using your partner's comments to guide you. This will be the final version for your school magazine.

Pulling it all together

Listen to extracts from essays written by members of your class.

Decide what are the key features that make these extracts effective. Be prepared to feed your ideas back to the class.

Set up to three targets for yourself for improving your next piece of discursive writing.

J The Art of Review Writing

How review text works

AIMS

- Explore the key ingredients of a review.

- Identify the main points, processes or idea in a text.

In this section you will think about what a review is and what features make a good review. You will read three reviews and discuss which one is the best.

Audience, purpose, form

A review is an evaluation[1] of someone else's work, such as a book, film or play. It is intended to inform and entertain the reader, as well as provide a personal opinion of how good (or bad) the subject of the review is.

Because reviews have so many different functions, they often combine aspects of several text types:

- **Discussion**, listing points both for and against the text

- **Persuasion**, persuading the reader to agree with your point of view, or to read the book, see the play, etc.

- **Information**, providing basic facts about the text.

evaluation – an assessment of the value or quality of something

TYPICAL FEATURES

The typical features of a review are listed below and on page 132. You will need to refer to these in Section 2.

- The **audience** is someone who is thinking of reading the book or seeing the film or play that is being reviewed. Sometimes they may simply want to be entertained or informed by the review.

- The **purpose** is to evaluate a book/play/film in an entertaining and informative way.

- The **form** or structure is often a series of paragraphs presenting different points, in a logical order, beginning with an introduction and ending with a conclusion. A review should include points both for and against the text before summing up the evaluation.

The Art of Review Writing

Typical **language features** of reviews are:

- lively use of language or humour to entertain as well as inform, e.g. an opening that grabs the attention like 'A rotten read'
- detail included, where necessary, to inform the reader about the text, e.g. 'The Rotten Romans' by Terry Deary/Series: Horrible Histories'
- conversational, informal tone to get on the side of the reader, e.g. 'Just when you've had enough of facts or descriptions'
- use of the third person when describing the text, and the first person when giving an opinion, e.g. 'Horrible Histories is a popular series ... I learned a lot.'

Task 1   Reading and annotating

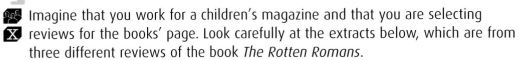

Imagine that you work for a children's magazine and that you are selecting reviews for the books' page. Look carefully at the extracts below, which are from three different reviews of the book *The Rotten Romans*.

- Identify the features of a good review in each of the extracts. The review with most of these features will go on the books' page.
- Discuss the weaknesses of the reviews that you rejected.
- Be prepared to explain why you chose the successful review and rejected the others.

Review 1

'The Rotten Romans' by Terry Deary

Series: Horrible Histories
Publisher: Scholastic
Illustrator: Martin Brown
Price: £3.99

'History with the nasty bits left in'.

Some of those nasty bits are:
- army massacres
- gladiator fights
- bloodthirsty emperors.

Other areas covered:
- Roman religion
- Roman food
- Roman games.

Layout and illustrations:
- usual format of the series
- includes cartoons, letters, news reports, quizzes
- cartoons vary in quality.

Review 2

'The Rotten Romans' by Terry Deary

'Horrible Histories' is the popular series of books on 'History with the nasty bits left in' – a promise (or a threat?) made by their creator, Terry Deary. 'The Rotten Romans' has more than the usual amount of nasty bits, so be warned. You would think that the Roman emperors would have set an example, but they were just as bloodthirsty as the masses who flocked to the circus to watch gladiators and wild beasts fighting horribly one-sided contests.

Blood flows in these pages, but killing isn't the only theme. I learned a lot about religion (surprisingly interesting), food (revolting), games (not so different from our own), and many other aspects of daily life. Terry Deary manages to bring the Romans to life, even though they've been dead for nearly 2000 years.

The layout of the book, which follows the usual format, is as varied as its contents. Just when you've had enough of facts or descriptions, up pops a cartoon, a 'letter', a quiz or a newspaper report to revive your interest. Some of the cartoons had me laughing out loud, though not all are this successful.

Review 3

A rotten read

'History with the nasty bits left in' is what it says on the cover, and how right it was. When my brother eventually lent me his copy of 'The Rotten Romans' by Terry Deary (almost a year after I had asked him – he must be the slowest reader in the universe) I found plenty of nasty bits in it. To begin with, some large insect must have got squashed between pages 18 and 19, spreading its juices far and wide and soaking into the surrounding pages. At least it added a bit of life (or should I say death?) to the description of executions that I think was underneath. The remains of my brother's pudding on page 58 were less in tune with their surroundings as they covered part of an interesting description of 'Caesar's sticky end' – and I'm sure it wasn't Death By Chocolate that finally did for him.

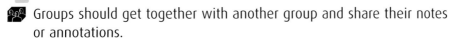

Task 2 **Discussing**

Groups should get together with another group and share their notes or annotations.

- Have you all chosen the same review for the magazine?
- Are your evaluations of the extracts similar? If not, why not?
- Discuss your conclusions and feed back to the class.

The Art of Review Writing

Composition and effect

Learning from example

AIMS

- Identify the main ingredients of reviews, and recognise how reviewers use language and organisation to achieve their purpose.

- Define and deploy words with precision, and use the context to work out the meaning of specialist terms.

In this section you will look in detail at a complete book review and analyse how it works. You will also test your knowledge of the specialist vocabulary that may be used in reviews.

Test watch As well as building up your writing skills, the following sections are good preparation for the optional reading tests at the end of Year 7 because they help you to:

- comment on a writer's purpose and the effect of the text on the reader
- comment on the structure and organisation of texts
- comment on a writer's use of language
- deduce, infer or interpret information, events or ideas
- describe, select or retrieve information, events or ideas from texts.

If you show these skills in the reading test, you will gain a better mark.

Task 3 Reading

 Read the book review below carefully. Consider what techniques the writer uses to engage the audience. Has she been successful?

**Caroline Lawrence,
The Thieves of Ostia,**

Dolphin Paperbacks, 2001, £4.99

> Precise details – inform reader about book at start

> Own experience – draws reader in

When I was given this book, I have to admit that I was a bit doubtful. 'The Roman Mysteries' it says on the front cover. **The real mystery, I thought, is why anyone should want to read about the stone dead Romans at all**. However, it didn't take me long to revise my opinion.   5

> First person – gives own opinion

> Humour – gets reader on side

The book may be set in Rome in AD79, but it's a fast-moving adventure mystery nevertheless, and like most books in this **genre**[1] it **makes** you want to turn the pages at a relentless rate: **I gobbled it up in only four sittings. The plot centres around a series of mysterious dog-killings (it is not for the faint-hearted as there is a lot of blood about)**, which are   10

> Third person – describes the text

> Conversational, informal tone

Whole
paragraph –
on the plot
and setting

Clear
summary –
gives the plot

Points for
and against
the feature

investigated by Flavia, the central character, and her friends. The author uses the clever technique of giving each chapter a **cliffhanger** ending, so you just have to keep reading to see what happens next. My only complaint is that the build-up is more exciting than the actual climax.

You might dismiss the characters as an ancient version of Enid Blyton's jolly nice Famous Five (they even have their own dog, Scuto) but you'd be wrong. Flavia is the well-to-do daughter of a sea captain, admittedly, but Nubia is an African slave girl, Jonathan is a Christian persecuted by his neighbours, and Lupus – the most fascinating character, in my opinion – is a beggar boy who has (literally) lost his tongue. Now that's not your usual bunch of kids. Yet they became my friends as well as Flavia's by the end of the book.

Setting the mystery in ancient Rome (or rather Ostia, Rome's sea port) adds a very important dimension to the story. As you read, you pick up huge amounts of information about the ancient Romans and how they lived – their houses, transport, food, customs and beliefs – yet this information seems to come naturally out of the story, so that you never feel you are being 'taught' as such. Some serious **themes** are dealt with on the way, too, such as the slave trade, poverty and multiculturalism. Although I was drawn into the ancient world of Ostia quite quickly, I think others may be put off by all the unfamiliar detail (despite the **glossary**, which helps a bit). There are lots of specialist terms, and lots of characters with very odd names. When Flavia swears 'Oh Pollux' under her breath, are we really not meant to laugh? I'm sure that wasn't the author's intention...

But this is a minor complaint about a book that really captured my interest from the first 'scroll' (as the chapters are called). The **blurb** promises further stories in the series, and the last page hints that the fearless foursome may soon be whisked to Pompeii. As Pompeii was destroyed by the eruption of Vesuvius in AD79, I think we are in for an explosive **sequel**. I look forward to it.

15
20
25
30
35
40
45
50
55

---

[1] **genre** – a kind or style of art or literature which has its own specific features, e.g. tragedy is a genre of drama, and science fiction is a genre of novels and films

Summarising the review

Task 4 — Topic sentences

 The topic sentences for the first two paragraphs of the review have been highlighted in orange.

- Identify the topic sentences in the rest of the extract.
- Decide how well they summarise the main points of the review.

Features of a review text

Task 5 — Annotating

 The first part of this extract has been annotated to bring out some key language features of reviews. Annotate the rest of the text to illustrate as many of these features as possible. Think about the effect of these features once you have identified them.

- The writer often uses the second person as well as the third and first persons. Why?
- What is the purpose of the final paragraph? Is it effective?

Using the right vocabulary

Books, plays, films and art exhibitions all have their own specialist vocabulary. It is important to be able to recognise this vocabulary and to be able to use it in your review writing.

Task 6 — Vocabulary

Seven specialist terms that are often used in book reviews have been emboldened in the extract and listed below. Write one sentence for each term to show that you know what it means. One has been done for you. If necessary, study the context[1] of the word in the review or look it up in a dictionary.

1 genre My favourite genre of writing is science fiction stories.

2 plot

3 cliffhanger

4 theme

5 glossary

6 blurb

7 sequel

[1] **context** – the parts of the text around the word or sentence focused on, which make the meaning clear

Advice on book reviews

  Discussing

Imagine that you are reviewing a novel aimed at 11- to 12-year-olds for your school magazine. The notice board below contains advice on things you should do in your review. Discuss this advice in small groups, and sort it into two categories: IMPORTANT TO INCLUDE and NOT IMPORTANT TO INCLUDE. Then rank the features you are including in order of importance. Be prepared to justify your decisions.

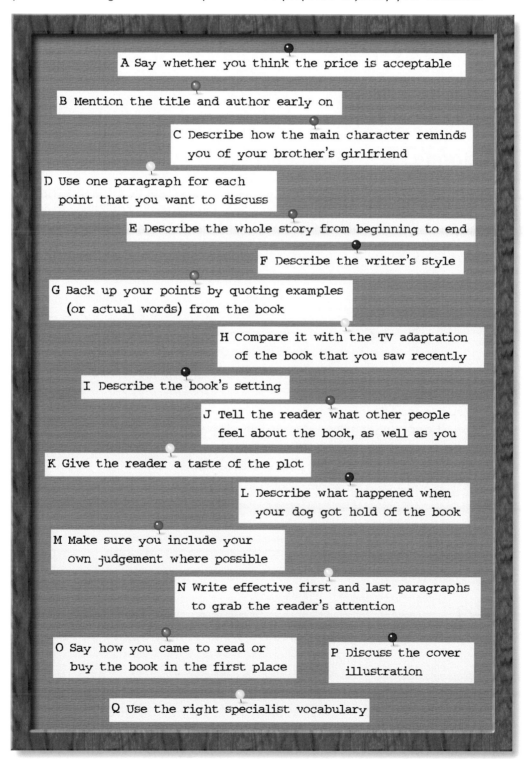

A Say whether you think the price is acceptable

B Mention the title and author early on

C Describe how the main character reminds you of your brother's girlfriend

D Use one paragraph for each point that you want to discuss

E Describe the whole story from beginning to end

F Describe the writer's style

G Back up your points by quoting examples (or actual words) from the book

H Compare it with the TV adaptation of the book that you saw recently

I Describe the book's setting

J Tell the reader what other people feel about the book, as well as you

K Give the reader a taste of the plot

L Describe what happened when your dog got hold of the book

M Make sure you include your own judgement where possible

N Write effective first and last paragraphs to grab the reader's attention

O Say how you came to read or buy the book in the first place

P Discuss the cover illustration

Q Use the right specialist vocabulary

Getting the structure right

AIMS

- Use a text skeleton to help analyse and structure a review, and think about how it should be paragraphed.

In this section you will investigate how the writer has structured the *Thieves of Ostia* book review, and explore how using paragraphs can make your writing hang together well.

Using text skeletons

In order to understand the structure of a text, it can be useful to draw a diagram or 'text skeleton'. Text skeletons represent the bare bones of a text. Using text skeletons will help you to analyse the structure of a text and to plan your own writing.

Task 8 ⬇ **Structuring**

👥 On page 131 it was noted that reviews often contain aspects of different text types.

Ⓧ Draw up a text skeleton to sum up the structure of the *Thieves of Ostia* book review,

TR with one person using an information skeleton and the other a discursive skeleton.

You may want to begin the information skeleton like this:

You may want to begin the discursive skeleton like this:

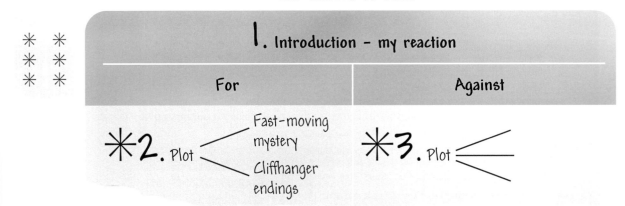

👥 When you have completed the text skeletons, discuss which is the more helpful way of analysing the review – or could either be used equally well? Be prepared to share your reasons.

Paragraphing

Paragraphs are an important way of organising your material and making it coherent and cohesive – see the explanation on page 56. As you can see, each main section of the information text skeleton relates to a different paragraph in the review. But is the order of the paragraphs important?

 Task 9 **Discussing**

Discuss the following questions.

- What order has the book reviewer chosen in her review?
- Could a different order have worked just as well?
- If you were going to cover the following features of a book in a review, in which order would you cover them, and why? (Characters, Themes, Summary of your evaluation, Language and style, Setting, Plot)

 Task 10 **Planning practice**

Plan a five-paragraph review of the book *Artemis Fowl* by Eoin Colfer. Read the ten sentences below. They include the first sentence of each paragraph and another sentence later in the same paragraph.

- Group the sentences into five paragraphs. Include an introduction, paragraphs on plot, characters, the writer's style and a conclusion.
- Finally, decide on the order the paragraphs should go in to make the most effective review.

A *Artemis Fowl* is definitely not like *Harry Potter* – it's more like *Die Hard* with fairies.

B He tries to blackmail the fairies into giving him vast amounts of gold, but he hasn't counted on Captain Holly Short of the fairy police force.

C I eagerly awaited the mixture of magic, school and adventure that had been promised.

D *Artemis Fowl* tells the gripping story of a clever 12-year-old boy (yes, Artemis is a boy, not a chicken) who discovers the secret world of fairies.

E It successfully mixes rip-roaring action writing, science fiction, wisecracking humour and high-tech funk.

F Artemis himself is a little unreal – he's too clever by half, and lives a life of luxury – though I like the way he isn't a goody-goody hero.

G But that didn't stop me enjoying a really good read, and looking forward to the sequel, as well as the film.

H *Artemis Fowl*, the first in a series by Eoin Colfer, was advertised as being a second *Harry Potter*.

I The fairies are intriguing characters, not the sweet little people in green tights that we know and love.

J The book is written in a very lively way.

Share your review structure and justify how you have arranged it.

The Art of Review Writing

Making the sentences work

AIMS

- Expand nouns and noun phrases to make sentences more interesting.

- Practise using the apostrophe.

In this section you will practise using noun phrases and noun clauses to liven up your sentence structure. You will also review the uses of the apostrophe.

Expanding nouns and noun phrases

GRAMMAR

Nouns can occur on their own or in **noun phrases**. Noun phrases, which are groups of words built around a noun, provide detail and clarity. Using noun phrases can make a sentence much more interesting and powerful.

There are many different ways to turn nouns into noun phrases. In the following examples the main noun in the noun phrase is 'book'.

- Adding an adjective before the noun, e.g. an <u>excellent</u> book.
- Adding another noun, e.g. a <u>children's</u> book.
- Adding a prepositional phrase, e.g. a book <u>on fishing</u>.

You can also expand a noun or noun phrase into a **noun clause**.

- The book was <u>lying on the ground</u>.
- The book <u>that I gave you</u>.

Of course, these methods can be expanded and combined to form longer and more interesting noun phrases:

- That short but excellent library book on fishing that I found lying on the ground.

However long and complex they are, noun phrases and clauses act just like a noun in a sentence. In the example below, the extended noun phrase (underlined) is all the object of the verb 'I have finished':

- I have finished <u>that short but excellent library book on fishing that I found lying on the ground</u>.

Task 11 **Recording**

 In groups of five, scan the book review of *The Thieves of Ostia* (pages 134–135) to see how many noun phrases and noun clauses you can spot (one person should read each paragraph).

- Be prepared to identify different kinds of noun phrase.
- Which are the most effective noun phrases/clauses, and why? Choose one from each paragraph.

The Art of Review Writing

The extract below is the first draft of a blurb for *The Thieves of Ostia*. Expand the highlighted nouns and noun phrases to make the blurb more interesting, and give it detailed description. Use as many of the methods outlined on page 140 as you can. For example, you could expand 'new series' by saying 'great new series from Dolphin Books'. You may also need to alter the punctuation of the extract.

> The Roman Mysteries is a new series for young readers. 'The Thieves of Ostia' has enjoyable characters and a mystery to solve. Themes include slavery, religion and poverty. A website and a discussion forum allow readers to ask questions. This is an excellent way to learn about the Romans.

Analysing apostrophes

GRAMMAR

There are two main reasons why we use apostrophes when we write: to indicate omission or possession.

1. Omission

An apostrophe shows where one or more letters have been omitted (missed out) from a word:

- He's late ('He' + 'is late' – the apostrophe shows where the 'i' has been omitted)
- We'll do it ('We' + 'will do it' – the apostrophe shows where the 'wi' has been omitted).

2. Possession

Apostrophes also show when something belongs to someone or something:

- Dad's car (the car belonging to Dad)
- Kevin's arm (the arm belonging to Kevin)

Top tip

1 The possessive adjective 'its' is an exception, as it does not have an apostrophe. 'The house and its garden' is correct.

'It's' with an apostrophe stands for 'it is'. The apostrophe is one of omission (a missing 'i'), not possession. For example, 'It's raining' is short for 'It is raining'.

2 Do not confuse apostrophes with inverted commas. Inverted commas look the same, but their job is either to show the beginning and end of direct speech (e.g. 'Oh Pollux') or to highlight a word or phrase (e.g. the first 'scroll').

Two of you are on the 'Possession' team, and two of you are the 'Omission' team. Scan the book review on *The Thieves of Ostia* (pages 134–135) together and identify each apostrophe. If it does the job that belongs to your team, award yourself a point. What is the score at the end of the game?

Task 14 Writing

Jamila wrote her first draft of a book review below without using apostrophes.

Rewrite the extract below to show where she should add them to make the writing clear and correct.

This books excitement level is high. If you dont like the idea of dogs heads in bags, then its not for you. The story is fast-moving and its setting is fascinating. Theres a lot of detail about ancient Rome and its clear that the authors done plenty of research.

5 Composing your own review

AIMS

- Use a text skeleton to plan, draft and revise a coherent information text that has been composed to suit a particular audience.

- Organise your ideas into coherent paragraphs using the first sentence to signpost the reader and developing and concluding them appropriately.

- Vary your sentence structure to add pace, variety and emphasis.

Your task

Write a review of a book that you have read recently, using all the techniques of good review writing that you have practised in this unit.

Test watch This writing task is good preparation for the type of writing required in your English tests because it helps you learn how to:

- plan your work so that it is organised logically into well-constructed paragraphs that are linked together well

- compose your writing effectively to match its audience and purpose,

- and select powerful vocabulary

- vary the structure of your sentences and punctuate them correctly.

If you show these skills in the optional English test at the end of Year 7, you will gain a better mark.

---

1 Audience and purpose

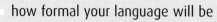

Choose a book that you have read recently and that you can remember well. (It need not be fiction.) Plan and write a review of this book for your school magazine. Remember, your audience will be students of your age or slightly older. The purpose of the review is both to inform readers about the book and to entertain them.

Discuss how the audience and purpose will affect the kind of review that you write. In particular, consider:

- how formal your language will be
- how you will both inform the reader and entertain them.

2 Brainstorming the content

Decide what you want to include in your review (look back at the checklist of important features on page 132). If you are reviewing a work of fiction, you could make notes under the following headings:

★ Plot   ★ Characters
★ Themes   ★ Setting   ★ Style

Then write topic sentences for each of these sections of the review.

⟨3⟩ Planning the structure

 Once you have your main points, the most useful planning tool is the text skeleton. Decide which skeleton (information, persuade or discussion) would best suit your review and use it to sketch out a plan.

Use your topic sentences to give you the main points for your skeleton. Then add notes on any extra points that you want to make in the form of memory joggers.

Remember to begin your plan with an introduction which grabs the reader's interest and end it with a conclusion which sums up what you think about the book in a memorable way.

⟨4⟩ Composing your piece

 Now you are ready to begin writing your review. It is always helpful to keep in mind the likely audience as you write. Read your sentences aloud every so often and ask yourself if they will be clear to your reader.

Points to remember

As you write, remember to:

- give your review a clear structure, with an introduction, a paragraph on each feature and a final conclusion (see page 139)
- think about the tone of your review – should it be formal or informal?
- provide a good balance of fact and opinion, using the third person for fact and the first person for your opinion
- give the reader a flavour of the plot
- include some specialist vocabulary to show you know what you are talking about (see page 136)
- engage the reader with interesting and powerful language (see page 136)
- write clearly and accurately, paying attention to your use of apostrophes (see page 141).

You may want to use some of the sentence signposts and connectives below to help you.

Sentence signposts and connectives

- A brand new adventure for
- Written for young teenagers
- Set in the year..., this thriller
- The plot centres around
- As for the main character
- The central theme of the story
- The author is at his best when
- The sentences are often
- but I felt
- So what's the verdict?

5 Peer comment

 • Swap your draft with your partner's and read each other's carefully. Discuss what works well and highlight this on the drafts. Then discuss how you could improve particular sections. Jot down your suggestions on the draft.

• Redraft the necessary parts of your review, using your partner's comments to guide you. This will be the final version to be submitted for your school magazine.

6 Pulling it all together

 • Listen to extracts from reviews written by members of your class.

 • Decide what are the key features that make these extracts effective. Be prepared to feed your ideas back to the class.

• Set up to three targets for yourself for improving your next review.

Exemplars

Key to Colour Coding

Orange	Topic sentences
Mauve	Time connectives
Red	**Connectives of opposition**
Turquoise	**Connectives of addition**
Pink	**Causal connectives**
Yellow	Simple sentences
Green	Compound sentences
Blue	**Complex sentences**

A — Narrative exemplars

Task 1 — Second half of tale:

Chronological order – helps reader follow story

Time connective – helps reader follow chronology

Powerful vocabulary – helps reader picture scene

> 'How long will it take me to get to Akshehir?'
> **When the Hodja did not answer even then, the man** decided he must be deaf, and so he started walking rapidly toward the city. Nasreddin Hodja watched <u>him</u> for a moment, and then he shouted,
> **'It will take you about an hour!'**
> 'Well, why didn't you say so before?' **demanded the man angrily.**
> 'First I had to know how fast you were going to walk,' answered the Hodja.
>
> *Traditional tale*

Third-person narrative – tells you who's telling the story

Dialogue – gives insight into plot and character

Past tense

Task 3

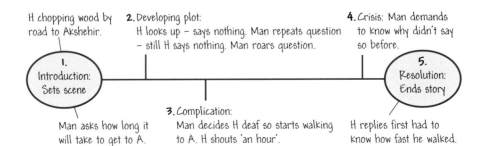

H chopping wood by road to Akshehir.

1. Introduction: Sets scene

Man asks how long it will take to get to A.

2. Developing plot:
H looks up – says nothing. Man repeats question – still H says nothing. Man roars question.

3. Complication:
Man decides H deaf so starts walking to A. H shouts 'an hour'.

4. Crisis: Man demands to know why didn't say so before.

5. Resolution: Ends story

H replies first had to know how fast he walked.

Task 6 From line 17:

Past tense ——

First-person narrative –
tells the reader who is telling the story

Time connectives –
to guide the reader

Chronological order – help reader follow story

'Anything,' I said. 'Didn't learn anything.'
'The teacher **spanked** a boy, though,' Laurie said, addressing his bread and butter. 'For being fresh,' he added with his mouth full.
'What did he do?' I asked. 'Who was it?'
Laurie thought. 'It was Charles,' he said. 'He was fresh. The teacher spanked him and made him stand in a corner. He was awfully fresh.'
'What did he do?' I asked again, but Laurie slid off his chair, took a cookie, and left, while his father was still saying, 'See here, young man.'
The next day Laurie remarked at lunch, as soon as he sat down, 'Well, Charles was bad again today.' He **grinned enormously** and said, 'Today Charles hit the teacher.'
'Good heavens,' I said, mindful of the Lord's name, 'I suppose he got spanked again?'
'He sure did,' Laurie said. 'Look up,' he said to his father.
'What?' his father said, looking up.
'Look down,' Laurie said. **'Look at my thumb. Gee, you're dumb.'** He began to laugh insanely.

Powerful vocabulary –
helps reader picture the scene

Dialogue –
helps reader picture character

Task 11

1st day	2nd day	3rd day	4th day	5th day
24 lines	13 lines	3 lines	1.5 lines	1 line
'The day Laurie started' – comes back rude	'The next day' – tells how Charles hit the teacher		Thursday – C pounded feet on floor – stood in corner	

'At lunch' – full of Charles's bad behaviour – rude to father

The third day – it was Wednesday of the first week – C bounces seesaw on girl's head – kept in

Friday – C threw chalk – lost blackboard priviliges

B Recount exemplars

Task 1 From paragraph 2:

Third person

Paragraphs –
organised in chronological order

Time connective –
helps reader follow order

Until the 19th century, **people** who owned watches had to check the accurate time by comparing the watch with a sundial. With new technology in the 1930s, quartz crystal clocks **were able** to keep time to about to about two milliseconds per day.
Today, the world's best timekeeper is the 'caesium atomic fountain' clock, which is **accurate** to **one second in 15 million years**.

Topic sentence – guides the reader

Past tense

Powerful vocabulary – helps precise understanding

Impersonal and formal language – to focus on the events

Task 3

1. 14C – Earliest mechanical clocks – accurate to 20 mins per day

3. Until 19C had to compare watch with sundial for accuracy

5. Today – caesium atomic fountain clock, accurate to one second in 15 million years

2. Mid-17C – pendulum clock invented – accurate to +/– 10 secs

4. 1930s – quartz crystal clocks accurate to two milliseconds per day

Exemplars

Task 5   From paragraph 3:

Paragraphs – organised in chronological order

Time connectives

Past tense

Powerful comparison – helps reader picture the scene

Topic sentence – guides reader

Powerful vocabulary – helps reader picture the scene

First person – this section is autobiographical

Formal language – suits purpose of text

The bronze orb that Atlas **held** aloft, **like the wire toy** in my hands, was a see-through world, defined by imaginary lines. The Equator. The Ecliptic. The Tropic of Cancer. The Tropic of Capricorn. The Arctic Circle. The prime meridian. Even then I could recognize, in the graph-paper grid **imposed** on the globe, a powerful symbol of all the real lands and waters on the planet.

Today, the latitude and longitude lines **govern with more authority** than **I** could have **imagined** forty-odd years ago, for they stay fixed as the world changes its configuration underneath them – with continents adrift across a widening sea, and national boundaries repeatedly redrawn by war or peace.

Task 9

Paragraph A – events related to first marriage

Paragraph B – events related to second marriage

1. H married Eliz Barrett 1718   3. Spring 1726 wife died   5. November 1726 marries 2nd wife (Eliz)   7. 1732 daughter Eliz born

2. Son John born 1719   4. Grief unknown – No diaries or letters   6. 1728 son (William) born – father's champion   8. 1737 1st son John died

Task 12   *Underlined phrases show uncertainty*

No one knows when or how Harrison first heard word of the longitude prize. Some say that the nearby port of Hull, just five miles north of Harrison's home and the third largest port in England, would have been abuzz with news. From there, any seaman or merchant could have carried the announcement downstream across the Humber on the ferry.

One would imagine that Harrison grew up well aware of the longitude problem – just as any alert schoolchild nowadays knows that cancer cries out for a cure and that there's no good way to get rid of nuclear waste. Longitude posed the greatest technological challenge of Harrison's age. He seems to have begun thinking of a way to tell time and longitude at sea even before Parliament promised any reward for doing so – or at least before he learned of the posted reward. In any case, whether his thoughts favoured longitude, Harrison kept busy with tasks that prepared to solve the problem.

Task 14   As Harrison lived near the sea, **he was probably aware of the Longitude problem.**

This is the only one of the subordinating conjunctions that can be substituted for 'because' or 'since' and maintain the same meaning. Some of the others make sense, e.g. When Harrison lived near the sea…However, this changes the meaning because it suggests that he moved away from the sea – a suggestion that is not made in the original text.

Task 16

1 Leon, a very good swimmer who lived near the sea, swam most days.
or Living near the sea, Leon, a very good swimmer, swam most days.

2 Julie, who was trying to find something interesting to watch on television, flicked from channel to channel.
or Julie, flicking from television channel to channel, was trying to find something interesting to watch.

3 Al, who had just woken up, peered sleepily at the clock, knowing he was going to be late again.
or Having just woken up, Al knew as he peered sleepily at the clock, that he was going to be late again.

C Information exemplars

Task 1 — From paragraph 2:

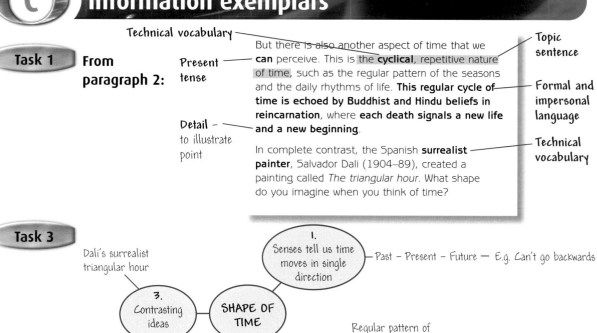

Technical vocabulary

Present tense

Detail – to illustrate point

> But there is also another aspect of time that we **can** perceive. This is the **cyclical**, repetitive nature of time, such as the regular pattern of the seasons and the daily rhythms of life. **This regular cycle of time is echoed by Buddhist and Hindu beliefs in reincarnation**, where **each death signals a new life and a new beginning**.
>
> In complete contrast, the Spanish **surrealist painter**, Salvador Dali (1904–89), created a painting called *The triangular hour*. What shape do you imagine when you think of time?

Topic sentence

Formal and impersonal language

Technical vocabulary

Task 3

Dali's surrealist triangular hour

What shape is time?

3. Contrasting ideas

SHAPE OF TIME

1. Senses tell us time moves in single direction — Past – Present – Future — E.g. Can't go backwards

2. Cyclical repetitive nature

Regular pattern of seasons

Daily rhythms of life

Echoed by Hindu and Buddhist belief in reincarnation

Task 5 — **From paragraph 5:**

Paragraphs – in logical order

Topic sentence – introduces key point

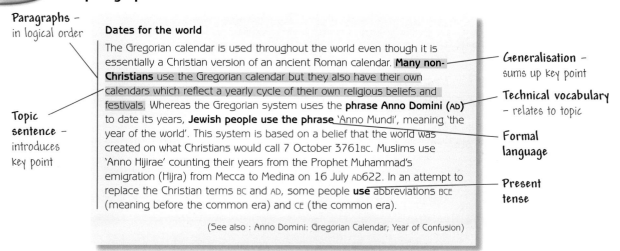

> **Dates for the world**
>
> The Gregorian calendar is used throughout the world even though it is essentially a Christian version of an ancient Roman calendar. **Many non-Christians** use the Gregorian calendar but they also have their own calendars which reflect a yearly cycle of their own religious beliefs and festivals. Whereas the Gregorian system uses the **phrase Anno Domini (AD)** to date its years, **Jewish people use the phrase** 'Anno Mundi', meaning 'the year of the world'. This system is based on a belief that the world was created on what Christians would call 7 October 3761BC. Muslims use 'Anno Hijirae' counting their years from the Prophet Muhammad's emigration (Hijra) from Mecca to Medina on 16 July AD622. In an attempt to replace the Christian terms BC and AD, some people **use** abbreviations BCE (meaning before the common era) and CE (the common era).
>
> (See also : Anno Domini; Gregorian Calendar; Year of Confusion)

Generalisation – sums up key point

Technical vocabulary – relates to topic

Formal language

Present tense

Task 11

The text in bold indicates a different wording from the original. Paragraphs have been used to mark the different sections.

The Muslim calendar is based on 'Anno Hijirae' because Muslims count their years from the Prophet Muhammad's emigration (Hijra) from Mecca to Medina on 16 July AD622.

However, the Gregorian calendar is used throughout the world even though it is essentially a Christian version of an ancient Roman calendar. Many non-Christians use the Gregorian calendar but they also have their own calendars which reflect a yearly cycle of their own religious beliefs and festivals.

Whereas the Gregorian system uses the phrase Anno Domini (AD) to date its years, Jewish people, **like the Muslims, do not use the Gregorian phrase. They** use the phrase 'Anno Mundi', meaning 'the year of the world'. This system is based on a belief that the world was created on what Christians would call 7 October 3761BC.

In an attempt to replace the Christian terms BC and AD, some people use abbreviations BCE (meaning before the common era) and CE (the common era).

Exemplars

Task 15 Because time is something which affects us all in many different ways, it generates some of the most intriguing questions asked by visitors to the Royal Observatory Greenwich, the 'Home of time'.

D Explanation exemplars

Task 1 From paragraph 2:

Present tense

Topic sentence – introduces key point

Structure – series of logical steps

Causal language – shows links

Technical, precise vocabulary

Structure – series of logical steps

> In June, the northern hemisphere of the Earth **is tilted** towards the Sun **causing** the longer, warmer days of summer. At the same time, it is winter in the southern hemisphere which is tilted away from the Sun.
>
> **When the northern hemisphere is tilted away from the Sun in December and January, shorter, cooler days are the norm**, and it **is** summer in the **southern hemisphere**.

Formal and impersonal language – including the passive

Present tense

Technical precise language

Task 2 Paragraph 1: Seasons caused by Earth tilting as it orbits Sun

Paragraph 2: When northern hemisphere is tilted towards Sun, it's warmer

Paragraph 3: When northern hemisphere is tilted away from the Sun, it's cooler

Task 3

North Pole always points towards Pole Star   Longer, warmer summer days   Shorter, cooler days

1. Seasons caused by Earth tilting as it orbits Sun

2. June – northern hemisphere tilted towards Sun

3. Winter – northern hemisphere tilted away from Sun

Winter in southern hemisphere   Summer in southern hemisphere

Task 4 From paragraph 2:

Causal language – shows how things are linked

Structure – series of logical steps

Topic sentence – introduces key point

Formal and impersonal language – including passive

> What many people do not realise is that the measurement of longitude (position east or west) is **directly related** to the measurement of time. The Earth takes 24 hours to complete one full revolution of 360°. This **means** that in one hour, the Earth revolves one twenty-fourth of a spin, or 15°, or that in 4 minutes it revolves 1°, and so on. This was an important fact for early explorers who found it impossible to navigate a ship while out of sight of land.
>
> To calculate longitude at sea, a navigator needs to know two things: what time is it on board ship, which **can be measured** using the Sun, and what time it is back home. The time difference converts into a longitude difference.
>
> Knowing the time back home was the biggest problem **because** there was no clock available which could cope with keeping accurate time on a rolling ship. **Many ideas were put forward for solving** the 'longitude problem' which was the greatest scientific puzzle of the age.

Present tense

Technical, precise vocabulary – relates to topic

Causal connective – to show how things are linked

Task 5

Feature that makes text easier to understand	Example
1. Using simple sentences to sum key points up clearly	Longitude is essential to the measurement of time around the world.
2. Using a formal but friendly style	What many people do not realise is
3. Referring to things the reader may already know	The lines of longitude and latitude are familiar from atlases and maps.
4. Using powerful words that precisely describe the process or idea being focused on (already highlighted)	pinpoint
5. Explaining technical vocabulary	one full revolution of 360°
6. Including examples to help the reader understand potentially complex points	or that in 4 minutes it revolves 1°

Task 8

Opening sentences or clauses of paragraphs	Role within text
Longitude is essential to the measurement of time around the world.	Topic sentence introducing the focus of the whole passage
What many people do not realise is that the measurement of longitude (position east or west) is directly related to the measurement of time.	Topic sentence introducing the focus of the paragraph and following on logically from the previous paragraph
To calculate longitude at sea, a navigator needs to know two things:	Topic sentence introducing the focus of the paragraph and following on logically from the previous paragraph
Knowing the time back home was the biggest problem.	Topic sentence introducing the focus of the final paragraph and relating back to the earlier paragraphs

Task 9

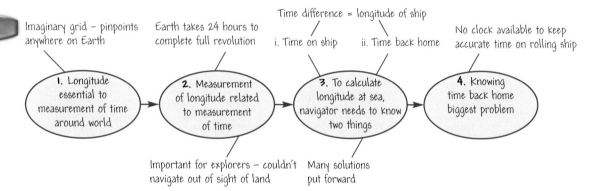

Task 10

Why the pupil got the simple addition wrong: The pupil got the answer wrong because she has jumbled up her tens and units. As you can see, instead of putting the 40 directly above the 97, she has moved it over to the right, causing it to be out of line. As a result, when she added the numbers up in the tens and units columns, she added in 4 rather than 40.

She should have put the 40 directly below the 59 and then added up all the units, followed by all the tens and finally the hundreds. Then she would have got the right answer.

Task 11

The mixture was heated until it was boiling. The length of time it took to reach boiling point was recorded; this process was repeated three times. Finally the experiment was written up.

Task 13

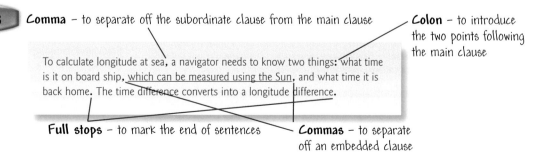

Task 1 From paragraph 3:

Formal English

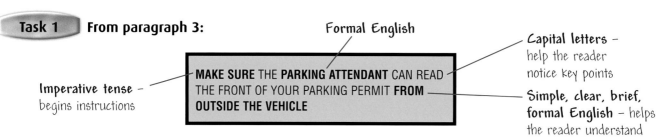

Imperative tense – begins instructions

MAKE SURE THE **PARKING ATTENDANT** CAN READ THE FRONT OF YOUR PARKING PERMIT **FROM OUTSIDE THE VEHICLE**

Capital letters – help the reader notice key points

Simple, clear, brief, formal English – helps the reader understand

Task 2

Scratch off five panels: day – date – month – hour – minute

Calendar faces outwards

From outside of car

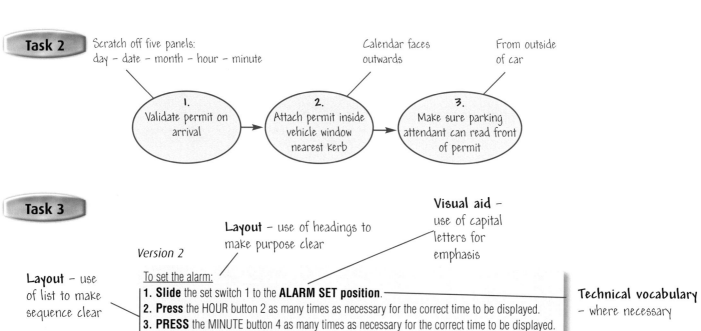

1. Validate permit on arrival

2. Attach permit inside vehicle window nearest kerb

3. Make sure parking attendant can read front of permit

Task 3

Layout – use of headings to make purpose clear

Visual aid – use of capital letters for emphasis

Layout – use of list to make sequence clear

Imperative tense – begins instuctions, making order clear

Version 2

To set the alarm:
1. **Slide** the set switch 1 to the **ALARM SET position**.
2. **Press** the HOUR button 2 as many times as necessary for the correct time to be displayed.
3. **PRESS** the MINUTE button 4 as many times as necessary for the correct time to be displayed.
4. **Slide the SET switch 1 back** to the run position.

Technical vocabulary – where necessary

Simple, clear, brief, formal English – helps the reader understand

Begins in direct manner – takes reader directly into centre of description

Alliteration – draws reader's attention

Task 5

Powerful verbs and adverbs – help the reader picture the scene

Figurative language (metaphor) – helps the reader picture scene

How not to set the alarm

In the pursuit of punctuality, a new alarm clock **beamed** by my bed. Perhaps I muddled up **the instructions for setting the time with those for setting the alarm**. I had spent some time **peering wearily** at the diagram and **cheerfully pressed** a few things in the misplaced hope that the alarm would sound at seven.

Romantic dreams **exploded** into the panic of reality when the alarm chose instead to wake at 8:30. I flailed at it in horror **like a drowning man. Detention loomed; even worse the relentless reprimands of a cynical tutor were already running through my mind.**

Relevant detail (but not too much) – helps the reader recreate the scene

Assonance – makes the description more striking

Figurative language (simile) – helps the reader picture scene

Varied sentence structure and punctuation – helps maintain the reader's interest

Powerful adjective plus alliteration – helps the reader picture the scene, plus alliteration

Task 9 Instructions for getting a cat into a cat basket

1 Find the cat basket and open it.

2 Put on protective clothing, especially gloves.

3 Take the basket into the room where the cat is and shut the door.

4 Pick up the cat, holding it away from you.

5 Put the cat inside the basket and only let go of the cat when you have almost shut the lid.

(F) Persuasion exemplars

Task 1 From paragraph 2:

Weasel words

Personal pronouns

Emotive idea – backed up by repetition of 'one book' and the exclamation mark

Emotive punctuation – use of exclamation mark

Emotive language

Direct address

So what's the catch? There isn't one!

All we ask is that, as a member, **you** buy **just one more book** from us in the next six months. **One book, that's it!** We're certain you'll want to buy more, but **the choice is absolutely yours** – we're that confident that you won't want to buy your books any other way!

No worries, we'll never send you a book you haven't ordered!

Once a month, we'll send you a **free magazine** featuring over 120 bestselling books. In the unlikely event you don't want to order anything, **no worries**, we won't send you anything you haven't ordered. We don't ask you to decline anything either, **so** there'll be **no nasty surprises or unwanted packages** on your doorstep.

Just pick up your phone now

Format (bold) to grab the reader's attention

Emotive language – to reassure reader

Logical connective – to show how statement supports the main point

Task 3 From point 2:

2. No catch

* One book in six months

Want to buy more

3. No worries

* Free magazine

No books you haven't ordered

No nasty surprises

Task 6 From line 17:

Form of statement (in capitals) and amusing repetition of 'billion' grabs attention

Direct address

Long sentence with exclamation – grabs attention at end of paragraph

Address http://www.travelbak.com/

Links

What is time travel?

Joining Travelbak™

FAQs

A history tour

How does your money grow?

The Time Travel Institute

Q. So how can this technology benefit me, exactly?
A. Well, we have established the Travelbak™ fund. A **small one-off contribution** to this fund, such as £100, will grow to an **incredible** £32 860 158 158 in 500 years.* (That's **32 BILLION pounds – yes, billion with a 'b'**.) **After deductions for administrative and legal expenses**, this fund will be used to give **you** that **time travel trip that you've always wanted**. Of course, the technology may be **dirt cheap** in 500 years. If it costs us only three billion pounds to take you into the past, then there's enough left over in the fund for you to live comfortably in your favourite era for several hundred years or more!

Q. What, can I go **anywhere and anytime** I want?
A. Of course, **we can't guarantee** exactly what the technology will be able to do in 500 years. However, we are confident that once the basic problem of time travel has been solved there will be **no barriers in time or space. Doctor Who, eat your heart out!**

Weasel words

Emotive word

Formal language – shows they are professional

Emotive words

Informal language – gets on reader's side

Rhetorical device: alliteration

Present tense

Emotive language

Informal language

Task 9

Q. Hey, what about travelling into the future – can I do that too?

A. Of course you can. The future will soon be past, after all! In 500 years' time we will literally be able to send you 'back to the future'. However, there are greater risks involved in this kind of time travel. If you put 'Neasden, 5 May 2450' on your form, we cannot guarantee that Neasden will be a fun place to chill out in on that date. So to insure yourself against any disappointment, why not simply take out our optional disaster insurance (£50)? This will refund your money in full if the destination you have chosen is troubled by nuclear holocaust or hostile aliens.

Task 10

From point 4:

4.
You can go anywhere, anytime

＊
Can't guarantee

But it will be possible

5.
Drawbacks

＊
Low health and wealth?

May alter course of history

Disaster may set technology back

Task 17

Dear _____

Are you aware of the threat that firms such as Travelbak represent to the public? Perhaps not. But I strongly believe that there should be a law against trying to extract money from people in this way. Many people do not know how to look after their money, and they need protecting by the law. Isn't that one of the main purposes of the law – to protect people from thieves? So please raise this issue in Parliament. The practice must stop.

G Argue exemplars

Task 1

From paragraph 2:

Question and answer – clearly introducing the next point

Use of third person rather than direct address

Connective – making a clear link in the argument

Formal language – shows the argument is serious

Connective – clearly answering the point just made

Sentence signpost – showing clear link to previous sentence

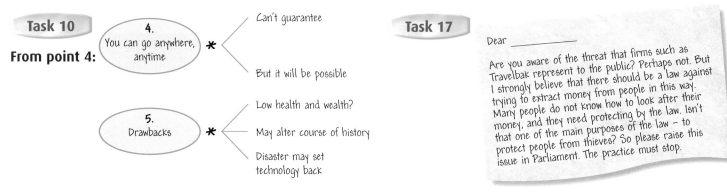

And what do MPs – our official representatives – plan to do about it? Well, nothing. You would think that MPs care about one of the most serious problems confronting society and would want to ask the government a few questions. Like: why is it that we are sending more and more criminals to prison, when **statistics show that people are more likely to commit further offences if they are sent to jail**? Isn't it meant to be the other way round?

So why have recent prison laws – at least one in each year since Tony Blair became Prime Minister – made prison sentences even longer and tougher? Only because a lot of voters think that tougher sentences are a **deterrent. But** tougher sentences are not a deterrent. **They may well deter those who are frightened by a spell in prison, but the prison population is made up of people at the very bottom of society. To these people**, the thought of 'doing time' is not such a big deal.

Reasonable tone and restrained language – doesn't put the reader off

Statistics – provide evidence for argument

Point – introduced in question and answer form

Connective – clearly answering the point just made

Further point – expanding on previous sentence

More evidence provided – to back up argument

Task 2

1 So why have recent prison laws – at least one in each year since Tony Blair became Prime Minister – made prison sentences even longer and tougher?

2 Besides, sending offenders to prison has the opposite effect to that which is intended.

3 For the majority, however, community sentences make more sense.

4 Doing time does not work – official

Task 3

From point 2:

2.
MPs are doing nothing

＊
They should ask questions

E.g. why use prison when prisoners commit further offences?

3.
Tougher sentences are not a deterrent

＊
Prison sentences longer and tougher

Voters think they are a deterrent

But they don't deter most prisoners

Task 7 Clever arguments

C: Those who say that old people are prisoners in their own homes are not facing the facts.

L: The evidence is clear in the official statistics: those most at risk of violence are young men.

E: For example, several young people were caught up in a gangland shoot-out at the weekend.

V: According to the NSPCC, the most likely victim of several crimes, from theft to murder, is a young person.

E: Several students in my form have been bullied – I don't think my form tutor has.

R: Most victims of mobile phone theft are young people, simply because they are the owners of the phones.

Task 11 The Home Secretary, therefore, should consider the reasons behind drug taking more carefully before he makes public statements on the issue. To present drug takers simply as bored does no justice to the facts. Often, as we have seen, young people are driven to take drugs for reasons beyond their control. They should be seen as victims, not criminals.

Task 13 **2** He was speaking after a New Year shooting in Birmingham when two teenagers were killed in a shoot-out.

3 In fact, only 0.12 murders per 100 000 people in Britain are caused by guns.

From point 2: **4** Violent gangster rap music was also criticised by politicians.

Task 15 Prisons throughout history have been harsh, grim places. Today's prisons still have quite strict regimes: prisoners have little privacy and no freedom, and there are many restrictions on their life. That is the price of their crime. However, modern prisons are not meant to be simply places of punishment. For example, they encourage people to study; outsiders and visitors are also allowed to come in; and writers take creative writing classes. The idea is to give the prisoners skills and knowledge, so that when they are released they are more likely to get a career. They are also less likely to end up in prison again.

H Advice exemplars

Task 1 From paragraph 2:

Softening the command

Informal tone

The only thing for it is to bite your lip when they're **stressing you out**. Instead of ignoring them, shouting at them or hitting them, get them on your side – believe it or not they can come in useful for all sorts of things.

Informal tone

Tell me about it

'My sister will go on and on until you kick her, then when she's sure there's something to see she rushes off screaming to my mum to show her.'

Philippa, 14

Speech bubble – used as a presentational device

Giving clear reasons for the last statement

Use of second person – for impact

What they'll come in useful for …

Subhead and bullets – as structural devices

- *Fetching and carrying your things*, e.g. drinks, snacks, your shoes, magazines. **Basically,** if you've got them trained correctly, you can send them off hunting for anything that isn't within easy reach.

Informal tone

The 'if' clause – gives reason to follow advice

- *Being used as decoys to distract your parents.* **If** you want to get **everyone off your case, send in Junior** to entertain and keep everyone occupied while you go about your business.

Informal tone

Informal tone

- *Sharing a laugh with when **your mates** aren't around.* Yes, believe it or not, if you make the effort to **spend some time with the little sprog, you may discover that he/she actually possesses something like a sense of humour.**

Informal tone

Humour – to get reader on your side

Task 3   **1** What they'll come in useful for...   **2** How to handle them...

Task 5

Try to remember that you are not living in a hotel. After all, there isn't a maid who comes round every morning to clean and tidy your room. If you insist on covering every square inch of floor space with rubbish your mum will definitely burst in and take over. How to prevent this? The only way is to tidy your room yourself.

It's hardly fair to say that, as it is your room, you can keep it as dirty and messy as you please. Your parents, brothers and sisters live in the house too, and you can't expect them to put up with a rubbish tip in their midst.

Task 6

From point 2:

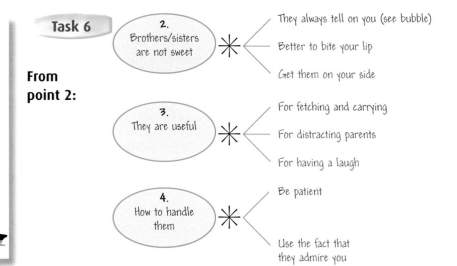

2. Brothers/sisters are not sweet
- They always tell on you (see bubble)
- Better to bite your lip
- Get them on your side

3. They are useful
- For fetching and carrying
- For distracting parents
- For having a laugh

4. How to handle them
- Be patient
- Use the fact that they admire you

Task 8

Manners do matter

- **Treat others as you would like them to treat you.** Stop and think about the effect of your words or actions – would *you* like to be on the receiving end of them?

- **Be respectful of others' feelings, needs and customs.** Just because you don't mind hearing a lot of swearing, does that mean other people feel the same?

- **Take time to be courteous and polite.** A 'please' and a 'thank you' cost nothing, but they buy you a smile and help to make a caring and respectful society.

Task 10

From point 2:

2 If she wants me to stay in, I'll be really fed up.

3 We will definitely have a row if she wants me to do my homework.

4 If we have a row, it'll end up with me storming off.

5 Unless I control my temper, it will make things worse.

6 She may let me out later if I butter her up first.

Task 12

Mum was in a bad mood for she was late back from work.

Whenever Mum was late back from work, she was in a bad mood.

Because Mum was late back from work, she was in a bad mood.

If Mum was late back from work, she was in a bad mood.

Having got back late from work, Mum was in a bad mood.

Getting back late from work, Mum was in a bad mood.

Mum, who was late back from work, was in a bad mood.

① Discursive exemplars

Task 1   **From paragraph 2:**

Sentence connective – showing point of view

Logical connective

On the other hand are the religious fundamentalists of a whole range of faiths, who **seek** explanations for **the world and all its works** in the holy book of their particular religion.
— Present tense
— Formal language

For example, in the late Middle Ages, **Christian scholars** tried to work out from the Bible how many years had passed between the making of Adam and the birth of Christ. They **concluded** that God had begun the six-day creation of the Earth on 23 October 4004BC. **This led to precise dates being added** in the margins of the Old Testament.
— Third person
— Formal language
— Impersonal language
— Logical connective

New paragraph – to show contrasting point

In the late eighteenth century, **however**, William Smith's investigations into the geology of the British Isles made him realise that some rocks were very old indeed, possibly stretching back millions of years before Christ. **His theories were dismissed by a society not open to new ideas.**
— Formal and impersonal language

Task 2

1 On the other hand are the religious fundamentalists of a whole range of faiths, who seek explanations for the world and all its works in the holy book of their particular religion.

2 For example, in the late Middle Ages, Christian scholars tried to work out from the Bible how many years had passed between the making of Adam and the birth of Christ.

3 In the late eighteenth century, however, William Smith's investigations into the geology of the British Isles made him realise that some rocks were very old indeed.

Task 3

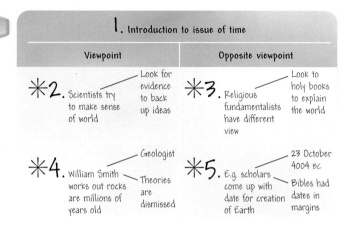

1. Introduction to issue of time

Viewpoint	Opposite viewpoint
✳2. Scientists try to make sense of world — Look for evidence to back up ideas	✳3. Religious fundamentalists have different view — Look to holy books to explain the world
✳4. William Smith works out rocks are millions of years old — Geologist / Theories are dismissed	✳5. E.g. scholars come up with date for creation of Earth — 23 October 4004 BC / Bibles had dates in margins

Task 5

From paragraph 3:

Sentence signpost
– showing point of view

Sentence connective

Sentence signpost
– showing point of view

Sentence connectives

Sentence signpost
– showing point of view

Present tense
and third person

According to most scientists, however, time and the universe were born in a gigantic explosion about 15 billion years ago – the so-called Big Bang. **The universe rapidly expanded from this fireball, then slowly condensed into galaxies; here, eventually life evolved from single-celled organisms.** There are three main pieces of evidence for the Big Bang theory. Firstly, the universe is still expanding today, as a result of the original explosion. Secondly, astronomers have found traces of the explosion in the universe. Finally, **the huge amount of certain chemicals in the universe, such as hydrogen and helium, is explained by the hot, dense period that followed the Big Bang.**

The creationists claim that they are not anti-science. **On the contrary, they say** that the Big Bang theory itself is unscientific, and breaks some of the most basic laws of science. **For example,** the total amount of energy in the universe should always be the same. **Yet** before the Big Bang there was apparently no energy at all! **The scientists admit** that the Big Bang doesn't follow the usual laws of physics, but **they argue** that in extreme conditions physics does not follow the usual laws.

Sentence connective

Formal and impersonal language

Present tense and third person

Sentence connectives

Formal and impersonal language

Present tense and third person

Sentence connective

Sentence connective

Formal and impersonal language

Task 6

Sentence signpost
– noun and verb, introducing the view

Logical connective

Supporting point

The scientists admit that the Big Bang doesn't follow the usual laws of physics, but they argue that in extreme conditions physics doesn't follow the usual laws.

Main point

Sentence signpost
– pronoun

Task 8

The creationists provide four main arguments to back up their claim that God, not the Big Bang, created time, life and the universe. The Bible is the main evidence, but the creationists also argue that the Big Bang theory is unscientific, that it doesn't explain why there are so many beautiful patterns in the universe, and that it does not provide a 'first cause' behind everything. Their arguments seem to me to be convincing. In particular, I cannot see how the universe could have come from nothing. 'How did time begin?' may be a big question, but the Big Bang is not, I think, the answer.

Exemplars

Task 9

From paragraph 3:

3 According to most scientists, however, time and the universe were born in a gigantic explosion about 15 billion years ago – the so-called Big Bang.

4 The creationists say that they are not anti-science.

5 The creationists say that if you go back to the start of the chain of cause and effect, there must be a 'first cause', which can only be God.

6 Creationists also point to the wonderful patterns and beauty of life in the world ...

7 Finally, creationists believe in the literal truth of the Bible, and nothing will shake that belief.

8 In conclusion, it seems as if scientists and creationists come from different planets themselves, as they hold such different views about the origins of time and the universe.

Task 11

1. Introduction — A big question — Conflict between scientists and creationists

Creationists	Scientists
✳2. God created universe — Either 10 000 years or billions of years ago / The Bible is evidence	✳3. Big Bang created universe — Still expanding / Traces of explosion / Explains chemicals
✳4. Big Bang unscientific — Breaks basic laws / E.g. amount of energy	✳5. Big Bang doesn't follow usual laws — But physics can do this
✳6. First cause must be God — Something must have caused Big Bang	✳7. No first cause before Big Bang — Big Bang was start of time and space

Task 14

1 Pessimists believe that the world faces a frightening future. For example, a disease like AIDS may infect increasing numbers of people. Furthermore, the earth may gradually overheat, making life impossible. Even worse, God may...

2 There are many conflicting theories about the end of the world. Some people think that a disease like AIDS may infect increasing numbers of people. Other people, however, say that the earth may gradually overheat, making life impossible. Religious people, on the other hand...

J Review exemplars

Task 1   **Review 2**

Informing reader of title and author at start

Conversational, informal tone – to get on the reader's side

First person – used to give own opinion

Each para on a different point

Conversational, informal tone – to get on reader's side

'The Rotten Romans' by Terry Deary

'Horrible Histories' is the popular series of books on 'History with the nasty bits left in' – a promise (or a threat?) made by their creator, Terry Deary. *The Rotten Romans* has more than the usual amount of nasty bits, so be warned. You would think that the Roman emperors would have set an example, but they were just as bloodthirsty as the masses, who flocked to the circus to watch gladiators and wild beasts fighting horribly one-sided contests.

Blood flows in these pages, but killing isn't the only theme. I learned a lot about religion (surprisingly interesting), food (revolting), games (not so different from our own) and many other aspects of daily life. Terry Deary manages to bring the Romans to life, even though they've been dead for nearly 2000 years.

The layout of the book, which follows the usual format, is as varied as its contents. Just when you've had enough of facts or descriptions, up pops a cartoon, a 'letter', a quiz or a newspaper report to revive your interest. Some of the cartoons had me laughing out loud, though not all are this successful.

Third person – used to describe the text

Lively introductory paragraph – to grab audience's attention

Powerful language

Clear writing – informing reader of content of book

Lively language/ humour – contrast between life and death

First person – used to give own opinion

Points both for and against a feature

Task 5   From paragraph 3:

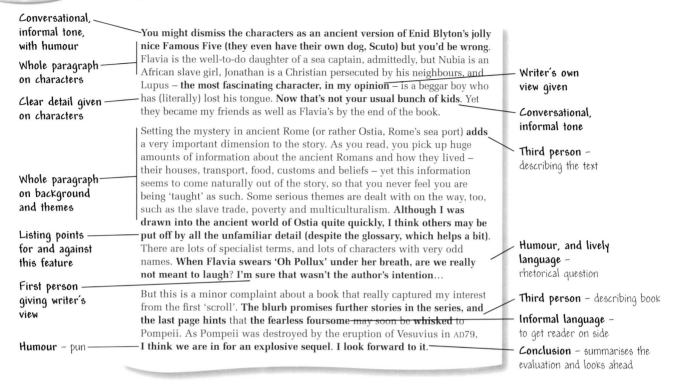

Conversational, informal tone, with humour

Whole paragraph on characters

Clear detail given on characters

You might dismiss the characters as an ancient version of Enid Blyton's jolly nice Famous Five (they even have their own dog, Scuto) but you'd be wrong. Flavia is the well-to-do daughter of a sea captain, admittedly, but Nubia is an African slave girl, Jonathan is a Christian persecuted by his neighbours, and Lupus – **the most fascinating character, in my opinion** – is a beggar boy who has (literally) lost his tongue. **Now that's not your usual bunch of kids**. Yet they became my friends as well as Flavia's by the end of the book.

Writer's own view given

Conversational, informal tone

Third person – describing the text

Whole paragraph on background and themes

Listing points for and against this feature

First person giving writer's view

Setting the mystery in ancient Rome (or rather Ostia, Rome's sea port) **adds a very important dimension to the story.** As you read, you pick up huge amounts of information about the ancient Romans and how they lived – their houses, transport, food, customs and beliefs – yet this information seems to come naturally out of the story, so that you never feel you are being 'taught' as such. Some serious themes are dealt with on the way, too, such as the slave trade, poverty and multiculturalism. **Although I was drawn into the ancient world of Ostia quite quickly, I think others may be put off by all the unfamiliar detail (despite the glossary, which helps a bit).** There are lots of specialist terms, and lots of characters with very odd names. **When Flavia swears 'Oh Pollux' under her breath, are we really not meant to laugh? I'm sure that wasn't the author's intention…**

Humour, and lively language – rhetorical question

Humour – pun

But this is a minor complaint about a book that really captured my interest from the first 'scroll'. **The blurb promises further stories in the series, and the last page hints that the fearless foursome** may soon be **whisked to** Pompeii. As Pompeii was destroyed by the eruption of Vesuvius in AD79, **I think we are in for an explosive sequel. I look forward to it.**

Third person – describing book

Informal language – to get reader on side

Conclusion – summarises the evaluation and looks ahead

Task 8   The information text skeleton suits the review better:

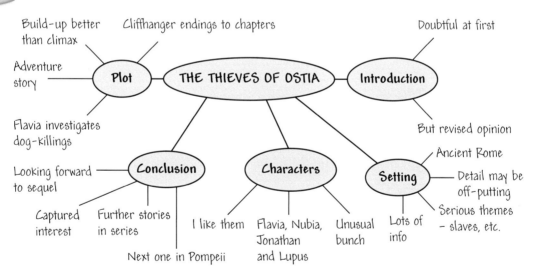

Build-up better than climax   Cliffhanger endings to chapters   Doubtful at first

Adventure story

Plot   **THE THIEVES OF OSTIA**   **Introduction**

Flavia investigates dog-killings

But revised opinion

Ancient Rome

Looking forward to sequel   **Conclusion**   **Characters**   **Setting**   Detail may be off-putting

Serious themes – slaves, etc.

Captured interest   Further stories in series   I like them   Flavia, Nubia, Jonathan and Lupus   Unusual bunch   Lots of info

Next one in Pompeii

Task 10
Paragraph 1: Introduction – H, C

Paragraph 2: Plot – D, B

Paragraph 3: Characters – F, I

Paragraph 4: Writer's style – J, E

Paragraph 5: Conclusion – A, G

Task 12

The Roman Mysteries is a **great new series from Dolphin Books** for young readers. The Thieves of Ostia, **which is the first book in the series,** has **many enjoyable characters** and a **gruesome mystery** to solve. **Some of the important and interesting themes covered in the books** include slavery, religion and poverty. A website and a discussion forum **devoted to the series** allows readers to ask **questions, which is an** excellent way to learn about the Romans.

Task 14

This book's excitement level is high. If you don't like the idea of dogs' heads in bags, then it's not for you. The story is fast-moving and its setting is fascinating. There's a lot of detail about ancient Rome and it's clear that the author's done plenty of research.

Published by HarperCollins*Publishers* Limited
77-85 Fulham Palace Road
Hammersmith
London
W6 8JB

Browse the complete Collins catalogue at:
www.collinseducation.com

© HarperCollins*Publishers* Limited 2004
10 9 8 7 6 5 4 3 2 1
ISBN 0 00 717762 3

Julia Strong and Kim Richardson assert their moral rights to be identified as the authors of this work.

British Library Cataloguing in Publication Data
A Catalogue record for this publication is available from the British Library.

Acknowledgements
The following permissions to reproduce material are gratefully acknowledged:

Extracts from *Aliens in Flares* by Maria Blyzinsky & Michael Barrett, first published by National Maritime Museum, 1999, reproduced by National Maritime Museum, pp24, 37, 39, 40, 42, 51, 53, 147; extracts from *Longitude*, reproduced by permission of HarperCollins*Publishers* Ltd © Dava Sobel, 1996, pp26, 28, 29, 148, 149; the parking permit is reprinted by permission of London Borough of Camden, pp63, 64; Westclox design is reprinted by permission of Salton UK, pp65, 66; *A Survivor's Guide to Families* by J Baker is reproduced by permission of Hodder and Stoughton Ltd., pp105, 106, 156; *Doing Time Doesn't Work*, adapted from the article *If It's Broke - Fix It*, by Chris McLaughlin, *The Big Issue*, April 28th-May 4th 2003. Reproduced by permission of *The Big Issue*, pp91, 92, 112, 154.

Whilst every effort has been made both to contact the copyright holders and to give exact credit lines, this has not proved possible in every case.

Project management by Lucy Hobbs
Edited by Nancy Candlin
Cover by ABA Design
Internal design by Ken Vail Graphic Design
Printed and bound by Printing Express Ltd., Hong Kong